PROLOG THROUGH EXAMPLES

by

I. Kononenko and N. Lavrač

SIGMA PRESS Wilmslow, Cheshire, U.K.

First published in 1988 by **Sigma Press** 98a Water Lane, Wilmslow, SK9 5BB, England.

British Library Cataloguing in Publication Data

Kononenko, Igor
      Prolog through examples.
      1. Prolog (Computer program language)
      I. Title II. Lavrač, Nada
      005.2'6   QA76.73.P7
      ISBN 1-85058-072-3

Distributed by
John Wiley & Sons Ltd., Baffins Lane, Chichester, West Sussex, England.

Printed by Interprint Ltd, Malta

Cover design by Professional Graphics, Warrington, UK

Reader Convenience Disc

A disc is available which contains all the solutions to the exercises from this book.

Solutions are written to be run under Arity Prolog for the IBM PC (or compatible) under MS DOS. Each solution is saved in a separate file; at the beginning of each file the text for a given exercise is provided as a Prolog comment.

Several of the programs also need:

- some input data in the form of a knowledge base
- some procedures defined in other exercises (references to them are provided as Prolog comment at the right hand side of a procedure call) or in text (such procedures are provided in the file TOOLS.ARI)
- operators definitions, at the top of the program
- the last sentence in a program must be terminated with a period and

Note also that Arity Prolog's syntax differs slightly from standard Prolog:

- operator // is used instead of div for integer division
- character ~ is not allowed to be used as an atom
- some procedures defined in exercises are already built-in Arity Prolog (length, findall)

However, users of other dialects will have very few problems in converting the programs.

A 5.25" PC-compatible disk as described above is available from Sigma Press for £11.50, inclusive of post and packing to the UK and Europe only. Other purchasers should remit £15 (or US $ equivalent) to include airmail despatch.

Sigma Press, 98a Water Lane, Wilmslow, Cheshire SK9 5BB, England

Preface

How can a novice Prolog programmer learn the art of Prolog programming? Just attending lectures or reading a textbook will not do. He has to do programming himself.

With this book we try to facilitate the reader's first steps into practical Prolog programming. Of course, we do not propose reading this book as a textbook only. The book should better serve as a useful guide when the novice Prolog programmer sits at a terminal or at a personal computer and tries to run the programs. This approach will enable him to get in touch with Prolog through practice. The book will lead the reader through a set of thoroughly chosen examples which will enable him to acquire the necessary programming skills, the required Prolog programming style and the feeling for the types of problems that are well suited to be solved with Prolog.

The book will be useful to students, programmers who are able to program in other computer languages, non-computer professionals who will find Prolog a simple and powerful tool for solving problems in their domains, and Prolog programmers who wish to improve their programming skills. It can also be used in any course of advanced programming languages. The only prerequisite needed for using the book as a useful programming guide is some basic knowledge about computers and familiarity with using some text editor, creating files, etc.

The book was designed to provide the reader – with numerous instructive examples that introduce the basic Prolog – concepts, a set of various exercises with solutions,
– explanation of typical Prolog programming techniques,
– examples that illustrate a good Prolog programming style and guidelines for program debugging,
– solutions to many practical problems that enable the reader to get a feeling for the kind of problems that can be solved with Prolog,
– explanations of the standard Prolog built-in operators and procedures, and
– a glossary of terms used in Prolog programming.

The book consists of seven chapters. Chapters 1–4 introduce the basic Prolog concepts through a series of examples. We suggest that these chapters are read sequentially. Chapters 5 and 6 give guidelines for effective programming in Prolog. They introduce some typical programming techniques, the appropriate programming style, as well as debugging techniques. At the end of each chapter we summarize the most important notions. Chapter 7 contains specific programs for particular problem domains given as solutions to more advanced exercises. Appendices A and B contain a list of standard Prolog built-in procedures and operators and should be consulted when programming. It is useful to glance over these two appendices to get a feeling of what are the features provided in Prolog. Appendix C contains a list of characters and their ASCII codes. Appendix D provides a glossary that may be consulted throughout the book. As in the field of Prolog programming there is a lot of diversity in terminology, the glossary is an attempt of its unification.

The book contains numerous instructive examples of programs. At the end of each section additional exercises are provided. The exercises are graded according to their difficulty: the more difficult exercises are marked by one asterisk (*) and the most challenging ones by a double asterisk (**), with comments on solutions to the difficult exercises.

Solutions to all exercises may be found at the end of each chapter. The reader should be aware that each programming task can have several correct solutions. We have tried to provide the best solutions by the following criteria: programming style, efficiency and logical clarity of programs. If the reader's solution is not the same as the one provided in the book it is not necessarily wrong. A comparison with the solution should make the reader think of other possible ways of solving the same problem. To verify that his solution is correct, the reader should run his program and the proposed program, and compare the results.

Programs in the book conform to the Edinburgh Prolog syntax, excluding syntactic peculiarities of different Prolog implementations. This syntax is an informally declared standard Prolog syntax, adopted by many popular Prolog implementations.

We are grateful to Damjan Bojadžiev, Neža Mramor-Kosta and Carl Uhrik who contributed significantly to this book by providing many helpful comments and advice. Many thanks to our colleagues Jordan Stojanovski and Igor Mozetič for their suggestions on earlier drafts of this book. Mario Radovan, Marko Grobelnik and Bogdan Filipič provided useful comments on particular parts of the manuscript. Ivan Bratko, the Head of the AI Laboratories at the Faculty of Electrical Engineering and the Jozef Stefan Institute in Ljubljana, introduced us to the field of Prolog programming.

Igor Kononenko, Nada Lavrač.

Ljubljana, 1987.

Contents

Chapter 1

Introduction to Prolog

Prolog is the programming language chosen as the basis for the new generation of computer systems. Based on mathematical logic, it enables the programmer to concentrate on the declarative, non-procedural aspect of programming. This is the main feature which distinguishes Prolog from other programming languages, thus representing a step in the development of automatic programming tools.

1.1 Prolog and Mathematical Logic

What is mathematical logic? In everyday life and especially in science when people disagree on certain points of the discussion, we often argue that our own statements are *logical* while the opponent's arguments are illogical. What do we mean by that? We mean that, unlike the opponent, we used rules of logical reasoning to derive our conclusions.

Mathematical or *symbolic logic* deals with rules of logical reasoning, i.e. rules of inferring conclusions from given statements. In the earlier stages of computer science mathematical logic was used only at the lowest level – to enable programming at the machine level. The last ten years have shown that mathematical logic can also be used on higher levels, as a basis of a high-level programming language.

Most of today's high-level programming languages (like Basic, Cobol, Fortran or Pascal) are not based on the principles of mathematical logic. These languages were developed to provide efficient computation and data manipulation. They enable us to use the computer as an effective tool for quick and precise computing and can serve as a 'reliable assistant' that is capable of dealing with a large amount of systematically organized data and can always efficiently find the desired information.

The new trend in computer science is to enable computers to handle more difficult tasks such as, for example, the simulation of experts' reasoning. Computer scientists have already developed many successful applications of *expert systems* that can intelligently solve problems in various domains. Expert systems can perform intelligent reasoning and can explain how they derive their conclusions.

1

The standard programming languages can be used to program expert systems, but obviously languages based on the principles of mathematical logic are much more appropriate for this task.

Up to now the most useful language of so-called *logic programming* is *PROLOG*. The name itself reflects the idea that the language is intended to enable *PROgramming in LOGic*. Prolog is usually introduced through formal logic. For practical programming in Prolog such formal introduction is not necessary. It is sufficient to state that Prolog is based on the first order predicate calculus restricted to Horn clauses that have the following form:

> *if* condition1 *and* condition2 *and* ... *and* conditionN *are satisfied*
> *then* conclusion *is true*

More precisely, Prolog clauses are extensions of Horn clauses, since Prolog also allows negative (negated) conditions. A Horn clause translated to Prolog syntax gives us the following Prolog clause:

```
conclusion :-
   condition1,
   condition2,
      .
      .
      .
   conditionN.
```

In Prolog, such a clause is called a *rule*. A clause without conditions is called a *fact*.

A Prolog program consists of a set of facts and rules that describe objects and relations between objects in a given domain. Facts are statements that are always unconditionally true, while rules declare properties and relations that are true depending on given conditions.

1.2 A Sample Prolog Program

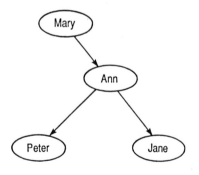

Figure 1.1 A simple family tree

Here is the corresponding Prolog program:

```
child( ann, mary).
child( peter, ann).
child( jane, ann).

parent( X, Y) :-
    child( Y, X).
```

The program consists of four clauses – three facts and one rule – each terminated by a period. The facts describe family relations. They state that Ann is a child of Mary and that Peter and Jane are Ann's children. The fourth clause is a rule stating that 'For all X and Y, X is a parent of Y if Y is a child of X.'

According to the Prolog syntax, names of relationships and objects are written with lowercase initials while uppercase initials are used for variables (X and Y in the fourth clause). In this program, names are *constants* as each name denotes exactly one person (one particular individual object). *Variables* in the program denote any person (any object) for which the relations defined in the program are satisfied.

A program must first be typed in by some text editor making sure that
– each clause terminates with a period,
– there is no blank space between a name of the relation and the left bracket of the arguments,
– there is a space before and after the symbol ':-', and
– the correct type of letter is used in names.

After the program has been stored on a file, e.g. named 'exercise', we can run the Prolog *interpreter*. This can be done with the following command to the operating system:

```
>prolog
```

The Prolog interpreter is ready when the Prolog *prompt* is displayed:

```
?-
```

Now Prolog is ready to execute our commands. Note that different Prolog implementations may require a different command for running the interpreter and also a different prompt sign may be displayed.

Our first command is to read in the program from the file 'exercise'. This can be achieved by typing the command 'consult(Filename)':

```
?-consult(exercise).
```

Note that there is no blank between 'consult' and the bracket '(' and that the command is terminated with a period. If Prolog finds any *syntax errors* in the program whilst reading it in

3

(e.g. if we forgot to type a period at the end of some clause) the interpreter tells us and we may exit by typing the appropriate command, e.g. 'halt':

```
?-halt.
```

After the program has been corrected using the text editor, the entire procedure of activating the Prolog interpreter and reading in the file is repeated. If there are no syntax errors in the program the interpreter answers 'yes' and is now ready for execution.

In the case of short programs, such as the one above, it is sometimes more practical to edit the program directly from the Prolog interpreter. Usually this is enabled by the command:

```
?-[user].
```

The program can now be typed in. When the typing is finished, <control Z> returns the control to the Prolog interpreter and the prompt '?-' is displayed again.

It is often useful to display the *current program* on a screen by the command 'listing':

```
?- listing.
child( ann, mary).
child( peter, ann).
child( jane, ann).

parent( X, Y) :-
   child( Y, X).
yes
?-
```

Now we can start the execution by asking questions about family relations. By means of *questions* we can ask what relations are true. We may want to know whether Ann is Mary's child.

```
?- child( ann, mary).
yes
```

Prolog answers 'yes' because this relation is found as a fact in the program. Questions always begin with the sign '?-' and terminate with a period '.'. Questions consist of one or more *goals*. The word 'goal' is used because Prolog accepts questions as goals to be *satisfied*.

Now we can ask if Ann is a child of Jane.

```
?- child( ann, jane).
no
```

Prolog answers 'no' as there is no such fact in the program. We can also ask Prolog who is Mary's child and whose child is Peter.

```
?- child( X, mary).
X = ann
yes
?- child( peter, X).
X = ann
yes
```

4

This time the answers are names that satisfy the relation in the question. Now we ask who is whose child in the given family.

```
?- child( X, Y).
X = ann
Y = mary;
X = peter
Y = ann;
X = jane
Y = ann;
no
```

Prolog lists all the pairs '(Child, Parent)', that satisfy the child relation. By a semicolon ';' we ask Prolog to give other solutions and it tries to find as many solutions as we ask it for. It answers 'no' when the goal in the question is not satisfied, i.e. when there is no alternative solution left.

We may ask Prolog who is Ann's parent.

```
?- parent( X, ann).
X = mary
yes
```

In this case, Prolog derives the conclusion that Mary is Ann's parent using the fourth clause in the program, i.e. the rule that defines the parent relation.

1.3 Prolog as a Step Towards Automatic Programming

The sample Prolog program partially demonstrates two important features. First, programming in it consists of describing relations between objects and not prescribing how the system should solve a task by a fixed sequence of instructions. And second, there is no distinction between data and program, between data retrieval and computation. In each case, we determine one or more arguments of a relation using the relations given by the program.

In these aspects, Prolog is substantially different from procedural languages like Basic, Cobol, Fortran or Pascal. When programming in these languages, a programmer's task is to translate a problem from its natural language specification – *what* is to be done (the declaration of the problem) – into a sequence of commands of a certain programming language that determines *how* to solve the given problem (proceduralization of the problem). In Prolog, the programmer's task is to translate the problem from its natural language specification into its formal logic form. A Prolog program thus determines *what* is to be done without saying *how*. A logical interpretation of a Prolog program is the following: Prolog accepts a set of facts and rules as a set of axioms and user's question as a theorem; it then tries to verify the theorem by logically deriving it from the set of axioms. An explanation how Prolog performs logical inferences appears in Chapter 4.

A further illustration of the above features is in the program below which computes the greatest common divisor of two numbers, using the Euclid's algorithm.

5

In Pascal, the solution of the problem is the following:

```
function DIVISOR(A,B : integer) : integer;
begin
  while A <> B do
    if A > B then A := A-B
             else B := B-A;
  DIVISOR := A
end; (* DIVISOR *)
```

In Prolog, the program is in fact a definition of the relation 'divisor'. It has three arguments and is satisfied if the third argument is the greatest common divisor of the first two.

```
divisor( A, A, A).
divisor( A, B, Divisor) :-
  A > B,
  A1 is A-B,
  divisor( A1, B, Divisor).
divisor( A, B, Divisor) :-
  B > A,
  B1 is B-A,
  divisor( B1, A, Divisor).
```

The program consists of one fact and two rules. As any other Prolog program, it can be looked upon in two ways: the declarative and the procedural. The *declarative* or descriptive reading defines the relations between given objects. On the other hand, the *procedural* or prescriptive reading determines how a program performs the task. We will explain both ways of reading the program by separately explaining each clause.

The declarative reading of the 'divisor' program is the following: the greatest common divisor of two equal numbers is the number itself (first clause); the greatest common divisor of two different numbers is equal to the greatest common divisor of their difference and the smaller number (second and third clause).

The procedural reading of this programs prescribes a sequence of operations for computing the greatest common divisor of two numbers: if the numbers are equal, the greatest common divisor becomes the number itself (first clause); otherwise it computes the difference between the greater and the smaller number and repeats the execution of the program with new arguments – the smaller number and the difference (second and third clause).

After the program is given to the Prolog interpreter, we may ask, for example, for the greatest common divisor of 24 and 30:

```
?- divisor( 24, 30, X).
X = 6
yes
```

The above program was used to illustrate the distinction between the declarative and the procedural meaning of programs. Besides, it shows how a relation may be defined in terms of itself, thus illustrating the use of *recursion* – the programming technique which is one of the features that make Prolog a powerful programming tool.

A programmer familiar to programming in *procedural languages* will wonder how describing relations between objects enables the computer to infer some solution or to perform a certain computation. In Prolog, the control mechanism which executes inferences is a part of the Prolog interpreter or compiler itself. Thus, given the necessary facts and rules, Prolog uses the built-in deductive reasoning mechanism to solve problems. In this way, Prolog represents a step towards *automatic programming*, whose goal is to enable the programmer to state only the specifications of the program and what is to be computed. The interpreter or the compiler of some future programming language will have to take care of how computations and inferences will actually be carried out.

Chapter 2

Basic Prolog Concepts

Prolog programs consist of clauses. *There are three basic types: facts, rules, queries and commands.*

2.1 Facts

Introducing Facts

In everyday life we often express facts about properties of objects and relations between objects. Here are three sentences that express some properties of objects:

> Blood is red.
> Summer is hot.
> John is fat.

The following three sentences express certain relations between objects:

> John is a son of Tom.
> Something is better than nothing.
> The living room, the kitchen and the bathroom are on the same floor.

According to Prolog syntax, these sentences may be written as the following *facts*:

```
red( blood).
hot( summer).
fat( john).
son( john, tom).
better_than( something, nothing).
same_floor( living_room, kitchen, bathroom).
```

In Prolog, properties and relations are expressed by *predicates*, each having a certain number of *arguments*. In the examples, 'red', 'hot', 'fat', 'son', 'same__floor' and 'better__than' are *predicate names* that denote properties or relations. On the other hand, 'blood', 'summer', 'girls', 'john', etc. are *arguments* that denote individuals. Prolog syntax requires that a predicate name is followed by a sequence of arguments enclosed in round brackets and separated by commas. Facts must always be terminated by a period. Note that there must not be a blank character between the predicate name and the bracket. The underscore character '_' may be used in longer names. In Prolog, the two natural ways of separating words – by using a space or a hyphen – are inadmissible.

Here are some more examples of facts:

```
child( jane).              % Jane is a child.

child( jane, ann).         % Jane is a child of Ann.

child( jane, ann, john).   % Jane is a child of Ann and
                           % John.

days_of_a_week( [mon, tue, wen, thu, fri, sat, sun] ).
/* The fact states which are the days of a week in their
   sequential order. Here we use square brackets - their
   meaning will be explained in the next chapter. */

sunny.                     % It is sunny.
```

In the above examples *comments* are introduced to explain the meaning of Prolog facts. Comments can be used to explain (a part of) the program, to describe a special programming technique that is used to solve a particular problem or to provide any other useful information about the program. Comments are ignored by the Prolog interpreter (or compiler) and serve only the person reading the program. In Prolog, comments are either enclosed in special markers '/*' and '*/' (which is useful for longer comments extending over more than one line) or are written after the percentage character '%' up to the end of the line (which is more practical for short comments).

Introducing Variables

In all of the above example facts, predicate names and arguments were written with lower-case letters. Predicate names must begin with a lower-case letter while arguments may also begin with a capital letter. In Prolog, capital letters have a special significance – they are used to denote *variables*.

So far, we have been using only *constants*, for example, 'blood', 'summer', 'john', 'something', etc. Constants are always denoted by names beginning with a lower-case letter. To express properties that apply to different objects or relations between objects in general, we use *variables*. For example, the statement

Everything has a name.

can be written as the following Prolog fact:

```
has_name( X).
```

X is a variable that stands for an unspecified object or individual and not for one particular object as in the case of constants. The fact 'has_name(X)' is read 'For all X, X has a name' because variables are *universally quantified*. Variable names begin with an upper-case letter. The same fact can be written as:

```
has_name( Everything).
```

Here are some more examples of facts using variables:

```
equal( X, X).              % Every X is equal to itself.

derivative( X, X, 1).      % For all X, the derivative of
                           % X with respect to X is 1.
has( X, mother).           % Everybody has a mother.
has( Person, father).      % Every person has a father.
```

Sometimes it is useful to use the *infix notation* in which predicate names are written between the arguments. In this way we can make it more readable as illustrated in the following examples:

```
3 < 5.                     % 3 is less than 5.

X = X.                     % Everything is equal to
                           % itself.
```

The above predicates '<' and ' = ' are *operators*. The definition and the use of operators will be explained in section 6.2.

Notes

1. Initially, the order of predicates' arguments is arbitrary but must be consistent with our interpretation and maintained throughout the program. For example, instead of:

```
son( john, tom).
```

we could also express the sentence 'John is a son of Tom' by the fact

```
son( tom, john).
```

although it is common practice in Prolog programming to keep the same order of arguments as in natural language. It is important to decide on the order of arguments and then strictly adhere to this ordering if we want to write Prolog programs correctly. Of course, in some cases, the order of arguments is completely arbitrary, as for example, in the predicate 'same_floor' above.

2. Like in natural language, in Prolog the same fact can be expressed in several different ways. The fact

```
red( blood).
```

could also be expressed by the fact:

```
colour( blood, red).
```

meaning that 'the colour of blood is red', or by the fact:

```
property( blood, colour, red).
```

meaning that a property of blood is that 'its colour is red'. The choice of an appropriate predicate depends on the problem we wish to solve.

3. A predicate is determined by its *name* and *arity*. The name denotes a relation and the arity of a predicate is the number of arguments in the relation. Thus, different predicates may have the same name but different arities. The form 'name/arity' is used when it is important to specify a predicate unambiguously. For example:

```
child( jane).
child( jane, ann).
child( jane, ann, john).
```

use three different predicates and express three different relations because of the different number of arguments. The first relation states that 'Jane is a child', the second one that 'Jane is Ann's child' and the third one that 'Jane is a child of Ann and John'.

On the other hand, 'child/2' is an unambiguous specification of the predicate with the name 'child' and two arguments. By this convention, the following three facts use the same predicate:

```
child( jane, ann).
child( [jane, peter], ann).
child( ann, 2).
```

Obviously, these facts represent three different relations. The first fact may state that 'Jane is Ann's child', the second that 'Jane and Peter are Ann's children', while the third one may say that 'Ann has two children'.

4. Syntactically, a fact is constructed from a single *positive literal* followed by a period. A positive literal is constructed from a predicate name followed by a sequence of arguments enclosed in round brackets and separated by commas. The infix notation can be used as well. Here are two examples:

```
derivative( X, X, 1).      % This literal is constructed
                           % with the predicate derivative/3.
3 < 5.                     % The predicate '<'/2 uses an
                           % infix operator notation.
```

Exercises

1. Translate the following sentences into Prolog facts:
(a) Judith plays the piano.
(b) John is a man.
(c) John is mortal.
(d) Everyone is mortal.
(e) Judith is sitting between Peter and Ann.

2. Tom and Ann are pupils. Mr. Richards is their teacher and Mr. Brown is the head-master of their school. Relations between them are given in Figure 2.1:

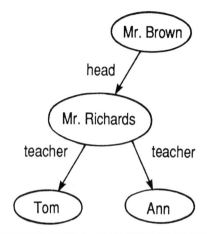

Figure 2.1 School relations.

Write Prolog facts describing the school relations using the predicates 'head/2' and 'teacher/2'.

3. Given the following facts:

```
is_a( tom, man).
is_a( jane, woman).
is_a( ann, woman).
is_a( man, human).
is_a( woman, human).
```

represent the relations that they describe in the form of a tree.

2.2 Rules

To express more complex relations as well as define new relations in terms of existing ones, *rules* are used. Here are some more complex English sentences:

If it is nice I will go for a walk.
If the weather is bad then take an umbrella.
No smoke without fire.

These sentences can be written as the following Prolog rules:

```
go_for_a_walk :- is_nice.
take( umbrella) :- weather( bad).
fire :- smoke.
```

Rules express properties or relations that hold if certain conditions are satisfied. The operator ':-' is used instead of the English 'if'. It denotes logical *implication*. We say that the left-hand side of a rule follows from its right-hand side. We call the right-hand side *the condition part* of a rule and the left-hand side *the conclusion part*. Like facts, rules have to be terminated by a period.

Here are some examples of rules using variables:

```
parent( X, Y) :-          % X is a parent of Y if
   child( Y, X).           % Y is a child of X.

nice( DAY) :-             % Any day is nice if
   sunny ( DAY).          % it is sunny.

buy( Person, Thing) :-    % A person will buy the things
   needs( Person, Thing). % that he/she needs.
```

Note that the same variable may appear on the left and on the right-hand side of a rule. Such a variable represents the same object. Note that the whole variable name can be written in upper-case letters (the variable 'DAY'). As in facts, variables in rules are also *universally quantified*. For example, the rule 'parent(X, Y) :- child(Y, X)' states that 'For all X and Y, X is a parent of Y if Y is a child of X'.

The condition part of a rule can be also more complex. Here are some examples of such rules:

```
nice( Day) :-                    % A day is nice if
   sunny( Day),                  % it is sunny and
   not_windy( Day).              % not windy.

buy( Person, Thing) :-           % A person will buy things
   needs( Person, Thing),        % if he/she needs them and
   price( Thing, Price),         % he/she can pay their price.
   can_pay( Person, Price).

neighbour( X, Y) :-              % X and Y are neighbours if
   address( X, Street, Num),     % they live in the same street
   address( Y, Street, Num1).    % but on different numbers.

older_than( X, Y) :-            % X is older than Y if
   born( X, Year1),              % X was born before Y.
   born( Y, Year2),
   Year1 < Year2.
```

The left-hand side of a rule always consists of one positive literal while the condition part may consist of one or more literals which can be *positive* or *negative*. A negative literal is a negation of a positive literal. Negative literals will be discussed in Chapter 4.

Literals in the condition part of a rule are called *goals*. They can be *conjunctively* (logical 'and') or *disjunctively* (logical 'or') connected. In case of a conjunction, goals are separated by commas and must all be true if the conclusion is to be true. In the above examples, we have only conjunctions of goals. In case of a disjunction, goals are separated by semi-colons and the conclusion is true if at least one of the goals is true. Here are some examples:

```
child( X, Y) :-              % X is a child of Y if Y is
   mother( Y, X);            % either the child's mother
   father( Y, X).            % or father.


take_umbrella :-             % Take an umbrella if it
   rains;                    % rains or snows or if it is
   snows;                    % cloudy.
   cloudy.


engineer( X) :-              % X is an engineer if he/she
   machine_engineer( X);     % is an engineer in some
   electrical_engineer( X);  % profession.
   biomedical_engineer( X).
```

Of course, conjunction and disjunction of goals can both be used in the same condition of a rule. Here are some examples:

```
grandmother( X, Y) :-        % For all X, Y, and Z, X is a
   mother( X, Z),            % grandmother of Y if X is a
   (mother( Z, Y);           % mother of Z and Z is either
    father( Z, Y)).          % a mother or a father of Y.


win_a_boxing_match( X, Y) :- % X will win a boxing match if
   knock_out( X, Y);         % X will either knock-out Y or
   (points( X, Px),          % if he/she will get more
    points( Y, Py),          % points than Y.
    Px > Py).


between( C, A, B) :-         % C is between A and B if
   left_of( C, A),           % C is left of A and
   right_of( C, B);          % right of B or
   left_of( C, B),           % if C is left of B and
   right_of( C, A).          % right of A.
```

As in logic, conjunction binds goals tighter than disjunction. Therefore, the brackets in the second rule are redundant and may be omitted while in the first rule they must not be omitted.

Notes

1. The usual convention when writing longer clauses is to write each goal in the condition part of a rule in a separate line and to indent it. This form clarifies the code and is easy to read.

2. If a rule contains a conjunction or a disjunction of goals in the condition part, same variables may occur in several goals. Such variables are called *shared variables*. An example of such a variable is 'Day' in the rule

```
nice( Day) :-
   sunny( Day),
   not_windy( Day).
```

The *scope* of the variable is the whole clause. The rule can be read as 'All days that are sunny and not windy are nice'.

3. Variables are universally quantified. But when variables appear only in the body of a clause, an alternative interpretation is possible. For example:

```
parent( X ) :-
    child( Y, X).
```

can be interpreted as 'For all X and Y, X is a parent if Y is a child of X', or equivalently as 'For all X, X is a parent if there is *some* Y such that Y is a child of X.'

4. A Prolog program consists of a set of facts and rules describing a domain, therefore it can also be seen as a *knowledge base* of an *expert system* for a certain problem domain. Facts are describing properties of objects and relations between objects of the domain. Rules are determining conditions under which certain conclusions about objects may be derived. Rules may also be seen as describing causal relations between objects. Solving a problem is done by querying Prolog whether a certain assertion can be derived from the program, i.e. whether a fact (or a conjunction of facts) is a logical consequence of the knowledge base of facts and rules. Opposed to other programming languages, a deductive inference mechanism is a part of the Prolog interpreter or compiler itself.

Exercises

4. Translate the following sentences into Prolog rules.
(a) Judith plays all the musical instruments that have a keyboard.
(b) Judith plays the instruments that both Peter and Ann play.
(c) Judith plays all instruments that Peter or Ann play.
(d) John likes anyone who likes wine.

5. Translate the following sentences from natural language into Prolog rules.
(a) Every man is mortal.
(b) (*) All men like all women.
(c) (*) All men like one woman.
(d) (*) Each man likes a woman.
(e) (**) Some people are smart.
(f) (**) Nothing is good and bad at the same time.

2.3 More Formal Definitions

Prolog programs consist of statements called *clauses* which are analogous to sentences of natural language. We have already introduced two types of clauses: facts and rules. A Prolog clause consists of a *head* and a *body* and generally has the following form:

```
head :- body.
```

The head of a clause consists of a single positive literal (or is empty) and the body consists of one or more literals called goals. The body can also be empty. Each clause is terminated by a period.

A *fact* is a clause that has an empty body. It is also called a *unit clause* and consists of a single literal, thus having the form:

```
p.
```

A fact declares a property or a relation that is unconditionally true.

A *rule* is a clause that has a head and a non-empty body. The simplest form of a rule is the following:

```
P :- Q.
```

Here P is the head, consisting of one literal, and Q is the body, which also consists of only one literal. In general, the body of a rule may consist of one or more literals conjunctively or disjunctively connected. Literals in the body of a rule are also called *goals* or *procedure calls*. Rules express properties or relations that are true if some conditions are satisfied. The body of a rule is called the *condition part* (or the right-hand side) and the head is the *conclusion part* (or the left-hand side) of a rule.

In general, a literal is constructed from a predicate name and arguments enclosed in brackets and separated by commas. A predicate name is chosen to describe a relation and arguments are used to describe objects in the given relation to each other. A predicate is unambiguously determined by its name and arity, i.e. by the number of arguments. If a predicate is also an operator then the literal has a slightly different form.

An illustration of all these notions appears in the following example:

```
lives( X ) :-          % X lives if X is a human,
   human( X ),          % if he/she breathes and if his/her
   breathes( X ),       % pulse-rate is greater than
   pulse_rate( X, N ),  % zero.
   N > 0.
```

The head of this rule consists of one literal, 'lives(X)', and the body consists of four literals, 'human(X)', 'breathes(X)', pulse__rate(X, N) and 'N > 0'. These four literals are also called goals. Each literal contains a predicate that describes a certain property or a relation. The literal in the head of the rule is constructed from a predicate 'lives/1' with the predicate name 'lives' and only one argument. The predicate '>'/2, denoting the relation 'greater than', is also an operator and is written between its arguments.

Exercises

6. What are the head and the body of the following clauses:
(a) boy(X) :- child(X), male(X).
(b) husband(X, Y) :- married(X, Y), male(X).
(c) lives(X) :- born(X), grows(X), multiplies(X).
(d) transitory(X).

7. Determine the literals and predicates used in the clauses of exercise 6. Which of the literals are goals?

8. Determine the predicates and the arguments of the following facts. Try to interpret these facts.

(a) `likes( X, mary).`
(b) `wants( X, money).`
(c) `famous_person( pablo, picasso).`
(d) (*) `lives( tom, address( stuttgart, hellerstrasse, 113)).`
(e) (*) `X > 0.`

2.4 Questions

We ask questions to enquire about some properties or relations that are of interest, such as:

Is Ann Mary's child?
Is Ann 15 years old?
Does Mr. Richards teach geography?
Does John love Ann?

We may write the above questions in Prolog as:

```
?- child( ann, mary).
?- age( ann, 15).
?- teaches( mr_Richards, geography).
?- loves( john, ann).
```

In Prolog, a *question* begins with the operator '?-' and terminates with a period. Questions are also called *queries*. We use queries if we want to retrieve information from the Prolog program. A query asks if a certain property is true or if a certain relation holds between objects. The answer to a query is 'yes' or 'no', depending on the facts and rules that constitute the Prolog program. In addition, questions may also include variables:

```
?- child( X, mary).          % Who is Mary's child?

?- age( ann, X).             % How old is Ann?

?- teaches( mr_Richards, Course).
/* Which course does Mr. Richards teach? */

?- child( X, Y).             % Who is whose child?
```

The Prolog interpreter will not only answer these questions simply with 'yes' or 'no', but will return *instances* of variables for which the goal in question is true. If Ann is Mary's child, the interpreter will answer the first question with:

```
X = ann
```

We say that the variable X gets instantiated to 'ann' or that the *value of a variable* X is 'ann'. We will further discuss the mechanisms by which Prolog finds answers in Chapter 4. Here we only mention that Prolog applies rules of logical deduction to find out whether the question can be inferred from the program.

In the above examples we used only simple questions, consisting of a single literal. More complex questions consist of a conjunction or a disjunction of literals as for example:

```
?- age( ann, X), X > 10.        % Is Ann older than 10?

?- teaches( mr_Richards, Course),
    class( a4, Day, Time, Course).
/* When and which course does Mr. Richards teach to the class A4? */

?- loves( john, jane),          % Do John and Jane
    loves( jane, john).          % love each other?

?- loves( jane, john);          % Does Jane love at least
    loves( jane, tom);           % one of the boys: John, Tom
    loves( jane, charles).       % or Charles?
```

A question is a clause that has only a body (and an empty head). As in rules, the body of a question consists of conjunctively or disjunctively connected literals. Literals in a question are also called *goals*. Unlike in facts and rules, variables in questions are *existentially quantified*. For example, the query '?- child(X, mary)' states that 'Is there such X that X is a child of Mary?'.

Note

In queries, a variable may occur in different goals. Again, as in rules, such variables are called *shared variables*. An example of such a variable is X in the question '?- age(ann, X), X > 10'. The scope of a variable is again the whole query. So we read the above query as 'Is there an X such that both goals age(ann, X) and X > 10 can be satisfied?' We can view shared variables as a means of restricting the range of variables of a simple query by additional conditions.

Exercises

9. Translate the following questions from natural language into Prolog queries:
(a) Which instrument does Judith play?
(b) Who can play the piano and the accordion?
(c) Does Judith play an instrument that has a keyboard?
(d) Does Judith play an instrument that both Peter and Ann play?
(e) Does Judith play any instruments that Peter or Ann play?

10. Translate the following questions into Prolog queries:
(a) (*) Does Judith play any instrument?
(b) (*) Can someone play the piano and the accordion?
(c) (*) Does anyone play any musical instrument?

Introduce and define a new predicate in order to avoid the use of the goal 'play (Person, Instrument)' as we are not interested in instantiations of variables that are not explicitly stated in questions.

2.5 Programs and Procedures

If we want to solve a certain problem in Prolog we first have to define it by a set of clauses called a *program*. A program consists of facts and rules, and questions are put by the user in order to find solutions to the problem.

Suppose we have the simple problem of deciding which car to buy depending on its quality. First, we have to select the interesting properties of cars. We may want to make a decision dependent on the following properties: fuel consumption (in litres per 100 km), acceleration (number of seconds needed to speed up to 100 km per hour) and price. Every car can be described by the predicate 'car' having four arguments (the first argument will be the name of a car). Suppose that we can choose between four cars:

```
/* car( Name, Fuel_cons, Accel, Price) */
   car( car1, 8, 10, 10000).
   car( car2, 6, 15, 8000).
   car( car3, 5, 10, 13000).
   car( car4, 9, 8, 11000).
```

The facts contain the necessary information needed to make the decision. Now we have to choose the evaluation categories. The two acceptable categories will be called 'very good' and 'good'. We will define these two categories regardless of the car price as that is a later decision factor. By the following rules we will define the predicates 'very__good' and 'good', each having two arguments – the name of a car and its price.

```
very_good( Car, Price) :-
  car( Car, Fuel_cons, Accel, Price),
  Fuel_cons < 6.
very_good( Car, Price) :-
  car( Car, Fuel_cons, Accel, Price),
  Fuel_cons < 7,
  Accel < 10.

good( Car, Price) :-
  car( Car, Fuel_cons, Accel, Price),
  Fuel_cons < 8,
  Accel < 13.
good( Car, Price) :-
  car( Car, Fuel_cons, Accel, Price),
  Fuel_cons < 9,
  Accel < 12.
```

The above clauses constitute the *program* for the decision making problem. The program is constructed from clauses grouped into *procedures*. A *procedure* is a definition of one predicate, i.e. a set of clauses that are about the same relation, containing the same predicate in their heads. In our example we have three procedures for three predicates: the procedure for 'car/4' consists of four clauses, the one for 'very__good/2' of two clauses and the one for 'good/2' also of two clauses. The program itself is not yet a solution to our problem; it is only the formal definition. In order to solve a problem we have to ask Prolog an appropriate question, which will force it to find the desired solution.

20

The goal is to find an acceptable car. For example:

```
?- very_good( Car, Price), Price < 12000.
/* Is there a very good car that costs less than 12000? */
```

Prolog answers 'no' which means that there is no car with such properties. As 'good' cars are also acceptable for us, especially if their price is lower, we ask Prolog another question:

```
/* Is there a good car that costs less than 11000? */
?- good( Car, Price), Price < 11000.
```

Prolog gives the following answer:

```
Car = car1
Price = 10000
yes
```

Notes

1. In the above example we used the variable 'Price' as a shared variable in a query. In this instance we showed how the use of shared variables in conjunctive queries restricted the range of variables by additional conditions. In our example, the range was restricted from all good cars to those good cars whose price is less than 11000.

2. Variables in different clauses are completely independent, even if they have the same name. We say, that the *lexical scope* of a variable is limited to a single clause. Each distinct variable in a clause should be interpreted as standing for an arbitrary unspecified individual. In the example:

```
grandmother( X, Z) :-
   mother( X, Y),
   parent( Y, Z).

parent( X, Y) :-
   mother( X, Y);
   father( X, Y).
```

we used variables X and Y in two clauses. In the first clause X stands for a grandmother and Y stands for a parent of Z. In the second clause X stands for a parent and Y for a child. Clearly, 'X' in the first clause denotes a different object than 'X' in the second clause.

Exercises

11. Define the following family relationships using the relations parent(Parent, Child), sex (Person, Sex) and brother__or__sister(Person1, Person2).
(a) mother(Mother, Child)
(b) son(Son, Parent)
(c) grandfather(Grandfather, Grandchild)
(d) uncle(Uncle, Niece)
(e) cousin(Cousin1, Cousin2).

12. For the school relations from exercise 2 illustrated in Figure 2.1:
(a) Define the procedure 'pupil/2' using the procedure 'teacher/2'.
(b) Define the procedure 'head/2' with arguments 'Head' and 'Pupil'.
(c) (**) Define the procedure 'superior/2' so that 'superior(X, Y)' is true if X is superior to Y. Note that X is superior to Y if X is his head or if he is a head of his head, etc. (Hint: see Figure 2.2).

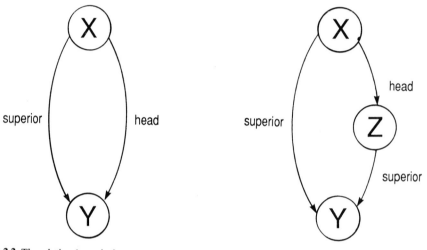

Figure 2.2 The relation 'superior'.

2.6 Commands

When programming in Prolog we can perform some operations before actually starting to solve a certain problem. For this purpose we use *commands*. We might wish, for example, to write something on the screen:

```
:- write( 'Hello').
```

We might want certain files containing Prolog programs and data to be immediately consulted (i.e. read by the Prolog interpreter):

```
:- consult( myfile).
```

Or we might wish to immediately run a program that starts with the goal 'go':

```
:- go.
```

A *command* is a Prolog clause. Like a question, it also has an empty head and a body consisting of one or more conjunctively or disjunctively connected goals. Although this is rare in practice, we may write several goals in one command, such as, for example:

```
:- write( 'Hello'), go.
```

The difference between a question and a command is that when a command is executed the resulting instantiations of variables are not output on a screen, while the resulting instantiations in questions are. Notions like execution and instantiation of a variable are explained in detail in Chapter 4.

2.7 Summary

– Prolog programs consist of a set of clauses grouped into procedures. A program defines the problem space by stating properties of objects and relations between objects. A procedure is a set of clauses that define a certain predicate.

– A clause has a head and a body. The head consists of a single positive literal and the body of a sequence of conjunctively and/or disjunctively connected literals, called goals.

– There are four types of clauses: rules, facts (with an empty body), questions and commands (with an empty head).

– A positive literal is constructed of a predicate name followed by a (possibly empty) sequence of arguments, enclosed in brackets and separated by commas. A literal in the body of a clause may also be negative (negated).

– We mark properties of objects and relations between objects with predicates. A predicate is unambiguously defined by the predicate name and the arity i.e. the number of its arguments.

– A command is a part of a program that is immediately executed. A question is usually not a part of a program and is used to force the execution in a dialogue with the Prolog interpreter.

– A comment is used to explain the meaning of a program, to clarify some special programming technique or to provide any other useful information about the program and is ignored by the Prolog interpreter.

– Constants are used to represent particular objects while variables represent unspecified individuals. In facts and rules variables are universally quantified and in questions they are existentially quantified. The lexical scope of a variable is a single clause.

2.8 Solutions to Exercises

1.
(a) plays(judith, piano).
(b) man(john).
(c) mortal(john).
(d) mortal(X).
(e) is_sitting_between(judith, peter, ann).

2.
```
head( mr_brown, mr_richards).
teacher( mr_richards, tom).
teacher( mr_richards, ann).
```

3. See Figure 2.3

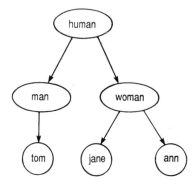

Figure 2.3 Representation of relations in the form of a tree.

4.
```
(a) plays( judith, Instrument) :-
      has( Instrument, keyboard).
(b) plays( judith, Instrument) :-
      plays( peter, Instrument),
      plays( ann, Instrument).
(c) plays( judith, Instrument) :-
      plays( peter, Instrument);
      plays( ann, Instrument).
(d) likes( john, X) :-
      likes( X, wine).
```

5.
```
(a) mortal( X) :-
      man( X).
(b) likes( X, Y) :-           % This is true for all X
      man( X),                % that are men and for
      woman( Y).              % all Y that are women.
(c) likes( X, woman) :-       % There is a 'Woman' that is
      man( X).                % liked by all men X.
(d) likes_a_woman( X) :-      % This is true for all X
      man( X).                % that are men.
```

(e) Existential quantification in facts and conclusions of rules can not be expressed in Prolog. We can overcome this problem by explicitly stating which persons are smart.

```
smart( einstein).            % It is necessary to state
person( einstein).           % that at least one person is
is_smart_person( X) :-       % smart.
   smart( X),
   person( X).
```

24

A simple solution (but, of course, not a very useful one) is to write the whole statement as a fact:

```
some_people_are_smart.        % or another possibility:
                              % smart( some_people).
```

(f) Negative knowledge cannot be directly expressed in Prolog. We can get a solution using a rule that will never succeed:

```
good_and_bad( X) :- fail.     % 'fail' is a built-in procedure.
                              % It immediately fails.
```

We can change our problem by explicitly defining what things are good and bad, using predicates 'is__good/1' and 'is__bad/1', and defining relations 'good' and 'bad' by using the built-in predicate 'not' (see Chapter 4).

```
good( X) :- is_good( X), not( is_bad( X)).
bad( X) :- is_bad( X), not( is_good( X)).
```

One could overcome the problem by literally following the statement:

```
nothing( X) :- good( X), bad( X).
```

6.
(a) head: boy(X)
    body: child(X), male(X)
(b) head: husband(X, Y)
    body: married(X, Y), male(X)
(c) head: lives(X)
    body: born(X), grows(X), multiplies(X)
(d) head: transitory(X)
    body: -

7.
(a) literals: boy(X), child(X), male(X)
    predicates: boy/1, child/1, male/1
    goals: child(X), male(X)
(b) literals: husband(X, Y), married(X, Y), male(X)
    predicates: husband/2, married/2, male/1
    goals: married(X, Y), male(X)
(c) literals: lives(X), born(X), grows(X), multiplies(X)
    predicates: lives/1, born/1, grows/1, multiplies/1
    goals: born(X), grows(X), multiplies(X)
(d) literals: transitory(X)
    predicates: transitory/1
    goals: -

8.
(a) predicate: likes/2
    arguments: X, mary
    interpretation: Everyone likes Mary.

(b) predicate: wants/2
   arguments: X, money
   interpretation: Everyone wants money.
(c) predicate: famous_person/2
   arguments: pablo, picasso
   interpretation: Pablo Picasso is a famous person.
(d) predicate: lives/2
   arguments: tom, address(stuttgart, hellerstrasse, 113)
   interpretation: Tom lives on the address Stuttgart, Hellerstrasse 113.
(e) predicate:'<'/2
   arguments: X, 0
   interpretation: Every number is greater than zero.

9.
(a) ?- plays(judith, Instrument).
(b) ?- plays(Person, piano), plays(Person, accordion).
(c) ?- plays(judith, Instrument), has(Instrument, keyboard).
(d) ?- plays(judith, Instrument), plays(peter, Instrument),
       plays(ann, Instrument).
(e) ?- plays(judith, Instrument),
       (plays(peter, Instrument); plays(ann, Instrument)).

10.
(a) plays(Person) :-   % In the answer we are not
       plays(Person, Instrument). % interested in knowing which
    ?- plays(judith).   % instruments Judith plays.
(b) plays_piano_acc :-   % In the answer we are not
       plays(Person, piano),   % interested in knowing the
       plays(Person, accordion). % name of the person that
    ?- plays_piano_acc.   % plays both instruments.
(c) plays_instrument :-   % In the answer we only want
       plays(Person, Instrument). % to know whether any person
    ?- plays_instrument.   % plays any instrument.

11.
(a) mother(Mother, Child) :-
       parent(Mother, Child),
       sex(Mother, female).
(b) son(Son, Parent) :-
       parent(Parent, Son),
       sex(Son, male).
(c) grandfather(Grandfather, Grandchild) :-
       parent(Grandfather, Parent),
       sex(Grandfather, male),
       parent(Parent, Grandchild).
(d) uncle(Uncle, Niece) :-
       parent(Parent, Niece),
       brother_or_sister(Parent, Uncle),
       sex(Uncle, male).
(e) cousin(Cousin1, Cousin2) :-
       parent(Parent1, Cousin1),
       parent(Parent2, Cousin2),
       brother_or_sister(Parent1, Parent2).

12.
```
(a) pupil( X, Y) :-
    teacher( Y, X).
(b) head( Head, Pupil) :-
    teacher( Teacher, Pupil),
    head( Head, Teacher).
(c) superior( X, Y) :-        % This is a recursive
    head( X, Y).              % definition. For more details
    superior( X, Y) :-        % about recursion see section
    head( X, Z),              % 5.1.
    superior( Z, Y).
```

Chapter 3

Prolog Data Objects

Figure 3.1 presents a complete classification of Prolog data objects. In Prolog, data objects are also called *terms*. Terms are either *simple* or *compound*. Compound terms are also called *structures*. Simple terms are either *constants* or *variables*. Constants are of two types: *atoms* and *numbers*.

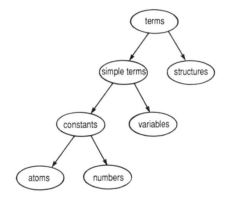

Figure 3.1 Data objects in Prolog.

3.1 Simple Terms

In Chapter 2 we already met various kinds of *simple terms* like:

blood, summer, john, kitchen, money, X, Y, 3, 15, Day, Px,
Py, geography, Course, Fuel__consumption, Car, Price, etc.

The reader may notice that these objects are of different types. Some of them represent one individual:

blood, summer, john, kitchen, money, geography

29

These objects are called *atoms*. *Numbers* are a second kind of simple objects:

3, 15

Atoms and numbers represent specific individuals, therefore they are called *constants*. Other simple terms are *variables*. Examples of variables are:

X, Y, Day, Px, Py, Course, Fuel_consumption, Car, Price

Variables denote arbitrary individuals, representing any object or a class of objects. Their value may change throughout the execution of a program. In Chapter 4 there is an explanation in detail on how variables get their values.

Let us see how simple objects are constructed.

Atoms

An *atom* is a constant constructed in one of the following three ways:

(a) Sequences of letters, digits and the underscore character '_'. They must start with a lower-case letter. The underscore character is often used to improve the readability. The following are some examples of atoms:

```
ok
judith
x25AB
george_washington
from_USA
series_no_2
```

(b) Sequences of special characters such as +, ¬, *, /, \, ^, <, >, :, etc. Some atoms have a predefined meaning. For example, the operators ':-' and '?-' are also atoms. Some other examples of such atoms are:

```
=
<==>
<--
::=
-&-
```

(c) Arbitrary sequences of characters enclosed in single quotes. This construction is especially useful when we want an atom to contain blanks or to start with a capital letter, otherwise not allowed, since capital initials are reserved for variables. Some examples of such atoms are:

```
'Ann'
'George Orwell'
'X & Y = Z'
```

Numbers

Numbers are the second type of constants. Depending on the particular implementation, Prolog may use integer and/or real numbers in a predefined range. The syntax of numbers can be seen from the following examples:

```
0
1984
-99
3.14
-100.001
```

In logic programming, real numbers are rarely used, as logic deals only with formulas that are either true or false. Despite this, many Prolog implementations support real numbers, which can be extremely useful.

Variables

A *variable* is a sequence of letters, digits and underscore characters starting with an upper-case letter or an underscore character. Except for the initial character, variables conform to the above rule (a) for constructing atoms. Examples of variables are:

```
X
New
Result
Street_No
_33_not
```

Occasionally, we are not interested in the value of a variable and don't want any name for it. For example, in the rule:

```
age( Name, Age) :-
   person( Name, Age, Address).
```

the address of a person is not of interest to us. Instead of the variable 'Address', we can use a so-called *anonymous variable*.

```
age( Name, Age) :-
   person( Name, Age, _).
```

When a variable appears in a clause only once, we are not interested in its value. In such a case we can use the anonymous variable denoted by a single underscore character '_'. An anonymous variable is used in place of a variable whose value is not of interest. The question:

```
?- child( _, ann).
```

reads as 'Does Ann have a child?' and the answer is only 'yes' or 'no'. The value of an anonymous variable is not output when Prolog answers the question. The question:

```
?- child( _, _).
```

is interpreted as 'Does someone have a child?'. Again the answer is 'yes' or 'no'. Note that two underscore characters function as two different variables.

Note

In a brief review of some properties of variables that were discussed in Chapter 2, variables in facts and rules are universally quantified except when a variable appears only in the body of a rule. In this case we may assume the existential quantification of a variable. In questions, variables are existentially quantified. The lexical scope of a variable is limited to a single clause, i.e. in different clauses variables with the same name denote in general different objects.

Exercises

1. Translate the following Prolog clauses into English:
(a) hates('Ann', 'Tom').
(b) sign('==>', implication).
(c) sign('&', conjunction).
(d) sign('*', Asterisk).
(e) can_spend(Ann, 10000) :-
    salary(Ann, X), X > 10000.
(f) can_spend(tom, _10) :-
    salary(tom, _20), _20 > _10.
(g) (*) hates(Ann, Tom).
(h) (*) ?- hates(Ann, Tom).
(i) (*) ?- hates('Ann', Tom).
(j) (*) ?- hates('Ann', _).
(k) (*) ?- hates(_, _).

2. Translate the following questions into Prolog. Use the predicate 'person/3' and assume that you have a set of facts in the form 'person(Name, Age, Address)'.
(a) How old is Tom and where does he live?
(b) How old is Ann?
(c) Who is ten years old?
(d) Does anyone live in Jamova street 39?
(e) Where does who live?
(f) Does anyone live anywhere?

3.2 Structures

Most real-world objects are *compound objects*: a person's name is made up of a first name and a family name; a date is composed of a day, month and a year; a dinner consists of an appetizer, a soup, a main dish and a dessert, etc. In Prolog, compound objects are called *structures*. These are appropriate for representing any objects whose descriptions consist of several components, for example:

```
name( First_name, Family_name)
date( Day, Month, Year)
dinner( Appetizer, Soup, Main_dish, Dessert)
```

To denote a structure we have to indicate what it represents by choosing a *functor* and put it in front of the names of the object's components. Components, enclosed in brackets and separated by commas, are called *arguments* of a functor. A functor is determined by its name and its arity, i.e. the number of arguments. Syntactically, a functor name is a Prolog atom and arguments are arbitrary Prolog terms: atoms, numbers, variables or other structures.

The above structures represent unspecified individuals from a class of objects described by the functor. We can replace variables with constants in order to address particular objects, for example:

```
name( john, richards)
date( 18, march, 1959)
dinner( pear_brandy, beef_soup, main_dish, cake)
```

Each component of a compound object may itself have an internal structure. For example, the main dish may consist of meat, vegetables, potatoes and salad. In a particular case we may have the following structure:

```
main_dish( rumpsteak, broccoli, cooked_potatoes, lettuce)
```

In this way the structure for 'dinner' becomes even more complex:

```
dinner( Appetizer, Soup,
   main_dish( Meat, Vegetables, Potatoes, Salad), Dessert)
```

A structure consists of components that can be broken down into further components. Of course, one always has to choose a special functor in order to combine components into a single object.

Another example of a compound object is that of a research paper that must conform to a standard structure in order to be published in a journal:

```
paper( Title, Author, Abstract, Contents)
```

Each argument may in turn be a structure itself, such as:

```
Author = author(name( Name, Fam_name),
              institution( Inst_name,
                           address( Place, Street, Number)))

Contents = contents( Introduction, Chapters, Discussion,
                     Acknowledgements, References)
```

From geometry we can give some other examples of structures. We choose the functors 'point/2', 'segment/2' and 'triangle/3' and use them for representing corresponding plannar geometric objects: a point with coordinates $X = 1$ and $Y = 1$:

```
point( 1, 1)
```

a segment between two points (1,1) and (4,4):

```
segment( point( 1, 1), point( 4, 4))
```

and a triangle determined by three points:

```
triangle( point(0,0), point(0,3), point(-5,-4))
```

Each Prolog structure can be represented in the form of a *tree*. The root of a tree is the functor of the structure and the nodes are its arguments. Nodes may be simple terms, represented by leaves of a tree, or structures, represented by subtrees. For example, in Figure 3.2 we have a simple tree that represents the structure 'writer(ivan, cankar)'.

Figure 3.2 A simple tree representing the structure 'writer(ivan, cankar)'.

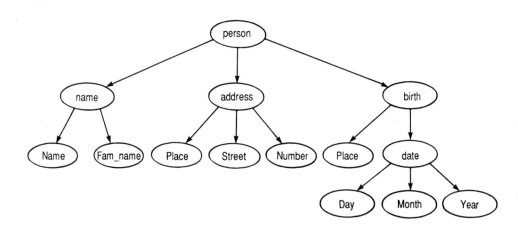

Figure 3.3 A tree representation of personal data.

Of course, the trees representing more complex structures are more complicated. For example, the structure describing a person by his/her name, address, and the place and the date of birth

34

```
person( name( Name, Fam_name), address( Place, Street, Number),
        birth( Place_of_birth, date( Day, Month, Year)))
```

can be represented as a tree in Figure 3.3. The functor in the root of the tree is called the *principal functor* of the structure.

Notes

1. In Chapter 2 we introduced literals as the basic constituents of Prolog clauses. Syntactically, a literal is a structure and the predicate used to construct a literal is a functor.

2. Each Prolog term is written as a sequence of characters. Characters are of four different types:
(a) upper-case letters A,B, ... , Z
(b) lower-case letters a,b, ... , z
(c) digits 0,1, ... ,9
(d) special characters * / ^ ~ : @ # ...

Prolog recognizes two kinds of characters: *printing characters* and *non-printing characters*. All characters listed above are *printing characters*, since they cause a mark to appear on the screen. Printing characters have ASCII codes greater than 32 ASCII codes of letters are arranged in alphabetical order. Therefore a simple comparison of ASCII codes allows us, for example, to sort items in alphabetical order.

Certain special characters have a predefined meaning. Some have been mentioned already: '%' marks the beginning of a comment; ',' represents the conjunction operator; ';' the disjunction; '__' indicates an anonymous variable. The meaning of other characters is explained in the following chapters.

Exercises

3. Write the Prolog structures given by the trees in Figure 3.4 (a) and (b).

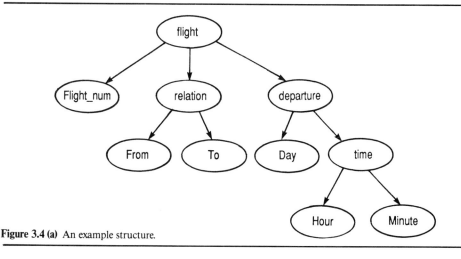

Figure 3.4 (a) An example structure.

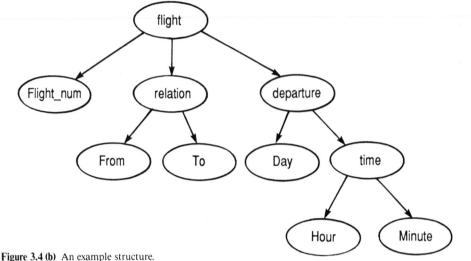

Figure 3.4 (b) An example structure.

4. (*) Suppose we have the following fact:
wrote (tom, sentence (pronoun (i), verb (love), pronoun (you)).What will Prolog
answer to the following questions:
(a) ?- wrote(tom, X).
(b) ?- wrote(tom, sentence(I, Love, You)).
(c) ?- wrote(Who, sentence(_, verb(Does), pronoun(Whom)).

3.3 Lists

A *list* is a Prolog structure used to represent an ordered sequence of items. For example:

[prolog, lisp, smalltalk, pop, snobol]

is a list of non-numeric programming languages and

[1, 2, 3, 5, 7, 11]

a list of some prime numbers. Elements of a list are written between square brackets and
separated by commas. In section 2.1 we have already used the list of the days of a week:

[mon, tue, wen, thu, fri, sat, sun]

Elements of a list can be arbitrary Prolog terms. Below is an example list of structures:

[bill(1, date(13, oct, 88)),
  bill(2, date(27, oct, 88)),
  bill(3, date(1, nov, 88))]

36

Elements of a list may also be lists:

```
[ [a,b], [a], [b], []]
```

A list with no elements is called an *empty list* and is denoted by ' [ ] '. The empty list is a Prolog atom.

A non-empty list consists of a *head* and a *tail*. The former is the first element of a list and the latter is the rest of the list, i.e. the list of all other elements. Some examples are:

list	*head*	*tail*
[a,b,c]	a	[b,c]
[[a,b],[a],[b],[]]	[a,b]	[[a],[b],[]]
[a]	a	[]

An empty list has no head and no tail. A list containing only one element has that element for a head and an empty list for a tail.

Lists may be written in a notation where the vertical bar ' | ' is used to separate the head from the tail:

```
[ Head | Tail ]
```

The above examples can thus also be written as:

```
[ a | [ b, c]]
[ [ a, b] | [ [ a], [ b], []]]
[ a | []]
```

The vertical bar can also be used to separate several elements from the rest of a list. For example, the same list can be written in the following ways:

```
[ a, b, c]
[ a | [ b, c]]
[ a, b | [c]]
[ a, b, c | []]
```

The operator '= ..'

The operator ' = ..' is a *built-in procedure* which can be used for constructing arbitrary Prolog structures. We introduce the operator through a series of example questions:

```
?- X =.. [ functor, arg1, arg2, arg3].
X = functor( arg1, arg2, arg3)
```

X is instantiated to a structure whose name is the head of the list and its arguments are the elements of the tail. This is further illustrated in the following two examples:

```
?- X =.. [ child, ann, jane].
X = child( ann, jane)
yes

?- X =.. [ name, billy, kid], Y =.. [ profession, thief],
   Z =.. [ gunman, X, Y].
X = name( billy, kid)
Y = profession( thief)
Z = gunman( name( billy, kid), profession( thief))
yes
```

The same operator can be used also in the reverse direction in order to obtain a list from a structure:

```
?- functor( arg1, arg2, arg3) =.. X.
X = [ functor, arg1, arg2, arg3]
yes
?- beatles( [john, paul, george, ringo]) =.. X.
X = [ beatles, [john, paul, george, ringo]]
yes
```

The operator ' = ..' can be used in both directions: to construct a structure from a list and to construct a list from a structure. When constructing a structure, the head of a list determines a functor and the elements of the tail determine the arguments of a structure, so the head must be a constant. Therefore, the arity of the obtained structure equals the length of a list minus 1.

Strings

For reasons of convenience, a notational variant is allowed for lists of integers which correspond to ASCII character codes. In this notation, a list of integers is written as a sequence of characters enclosed in double quotes. For example:

```
"PROLOG" = [ 80, 82, 79, 76, 79, 71]
```

Lists written in this notation are called *strings*.

A useful built-in procedure which transforms strings into corresponding atoms, and vice versa, is 'name(Atom, String)'. The following dialogue illustrates its use:

```
?- name( X, [ 80, 82, 79, 76, 79, 71]).
X = 'PROLOG'
yes
?- name( triglav, X).
X = [ 116, 114, 105, 103, 108, 97, 118]
yes
?- name( X, "PROLOG THROUGH EXAMPLES").
X = 'PROLOG THROUGH EXAMPLES'
yes
```

Notes

1. We can represent lists in a way similar to all other Prolog structures by using a special functor named 'dot' and denoted by ' . '. The two arguments of the 'dot' functor are the head and the tail of a list, i.e.

```
.( Head, Tail)
```

A list can be represented in the form of a tree in Figure 3.5.

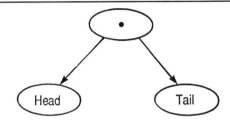

Figure 3.5 A list represented in the form of a tree.

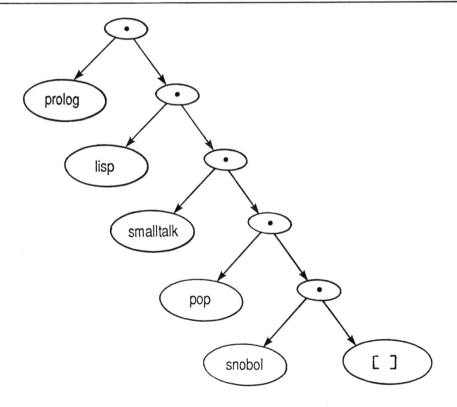

Figure 3.6 A list of non-numeric programming languages represented in the form of a tree.

A list of non-numeric programming languages

```
[prolog, lisp, smalltalk, pop, snobol]
```

can thus be rewritten as the following structure:

```
.(prolog,.(lisp,.(smalltalk,.(pop,.(snobol,[])))))
```

and can be represented by the tree in Figure 3.6.

By using the 'dot' notation, we obtain the same representation for lists as for other Prolog structures. Each non-empty list is a structure with '.' as its functor and the head and the tail of a list as its arguments.

It is obviously much more convenient to use the square bracket notation than the dot notation for lists. The representation with the functor '.' is used internally by the interpreter. The square bracket notation is commonly used by programmers and by Prolog when it outputs lists.

2. Lists are often used to represent sets. However, there is a substantial difference between sets and lists. In a set, each element occurs only once and the ordering of elements is arbitrary. On the other hand, a list has a defined sequential order of items and items may also occur in a list more than once. Thus, the same set, for example the set of elements a, b and c, can be represented by several lists:

```
[a, b, c], [b, a, c], [b, c, a], etc.
```

Certain lists do not represent sets, for example:

```
[a, a, a, b, b]
```

The empty list '[ ]' denotes the empty set.

3. As we mentioned above, the vertical bar can be used to separate some elements of a list from the rest of the list. This notation is very useful because it enables dealing with unbounded lists. For example, let us have the following list of prime numbers:

```
[ 1, 2, 3, 5, 7 | Tail]
```

If later, during the execution of some program, the tail 'Tail' is given the value '[11 | Tail1]' i.e. if

```
Tail = [ 11 | Tail1]
```

we obtain the list

```
[ 1, 2, 3, 5, 7 | [ 11 | Tail1]] = [ 1, 2, 3, 5, 7, 11 | Tail1]
```

which is again unbounded. As such, it can be lengthened during the further execution of the program. This enables us to deal with unbounded sets of elements.

4. Lists, as one of the most important Prolog structures, are widely used in non-numeric programming. We should mention that lists are the basic data structure of the programming language LISP. They can be used to represent arbitrarily complex structures. However, sometimes it is more convenient to use different structures.

In this section we introduced only the basic list notation and gave some simple examples of lists. More complicated operations on lists will be dealt with in section 5.2.

Exercises

5. What are the heads and the tails of the following lists:
(a) [a, b, c, d]
(b) [a, b | X]
(c) [X | Y]
(d) [X | [Y]]
(e) [a| b]
(f) [X]
(g) X
(h) [[a, b, c| d], e| [f, g| X]]
(i) []
(j) [a| [b|[c| [d]]]]

6. (*) Suppose we have the following fact: 'separate([Head | Tail], Head, Tail)'. What will Prolog answer to the following questions:
(a) ?- separate([a, b, c], H, T).
(b) ?- separate(L, a, [b, c]).
(c) ?- separate([a | T], H, []).
(d) ?- separate(L, [a], [a]).
(e) ?- separate([[] | T], H, H).
(f) ?- separate([a, b | T], H, [b, c, d]).
(g) (**) ?- separate(L, a, b).
(h) (**) ?- separate(L, a, T), separate(T, b, T1),
    separate(T1, c, []).
(i) (**) ?- separate([], H, T).

7.
(a) (*) Define the third element of a list in the form
    'third_element(X, List)'.
(b) (**) Define the last element of a list in the form
    'last_element(X, List)'.

8. Translate the following sentences into Prolog, assuming that the valid functors are defined with facts in the form 'function__symbol(Name, Arity)' and valid predicates with facts of the form 'predicate(Name, Arity)':
(a) (**)
    Rule 1: A constant is a term.
    Rule 2: A variable is a term.
    Rule 3: If f is a n-ary function synbol (functor) and if for n > =1 t1, ..., tn are terms, then
        f(t1, ..., tn) is also a term.

The only way of constructing terms is by rules 1, 2 and 3. (Hint: Use the built-in procedures '= ..', 'var/1', 'atomic/1' and 'length/2', see Appendix A.)
(b) (**)
 If P is an n-ary predicate and if for n >= 1 t1, ..., tn are terms, then P(t1, ..., tn) is an atomic formula.
(c) If A is an atomic formula, then A and not(A) are literals.

3.4 Arithmetic

When programming in Prolog, we are mainly concerned with logical reasoning and symbolic computations. Still, we sometimes need to do numerical computing. Prolog enables us to evaluate arithmetic expressions by using the built-in procedure 'is' which is an infix operator. For example, we can ask Prolog to compute the sum of two numbers, such as

```
?- X is 2 + 3.
```

and the answer will be

```
X = 5
yes
```

The following dialogue with the Prolog interpreter illustrates some Prolog features when doing arithmetic computations:

```
?- X is 17 div 3.          % 'div' denotes integer division.
X = 5
yes
?- X is 2 + 3 * (17 div 3).
X = 17
yes
?- X is 17 - (18 / 5).
X = 13.4
yes
?- X is 17 mod 3.          % 'mod' denotes remainder of integer division.
X = 2
yes
?- 5 is 2 + 3.
yes
?- 4 is 2 + 3.
no
?- 2 + 3 is 2 + 3.
no
```

The operator 'is' evaluates the expression at the right-hand side. If the left-hand side of the 'is' operator is a variable then its value is set to the computed value. If the left-hand side is a number or a variable that already has a value, the result is compared with this number. The answer is 'yes' if both numbers are identical and 'no' otherwise.

Arithmetic expressions are Prolog structures that use *arithmetic operators*. They are written in a special notation which improves readability. For example, the expression:

```
2 + 3 * (17 div 3)
```

can be used in place of the expression in the standard Prolog notation:

```
+( 2, *( 3, div( 17, 3)))
```

The arithmetic expressions in the above examples are structures using the functors ' + ', ' − ', '*', '/', 'mod' and 'div', each with two arguments. These functors are *built-in operators* and are usually written in the *infix* notation (i.e. between two arguments) in order to improve readability. For more details about operators see section 6.2. Each operator has a certain *precedence* that defines the strength of the operator binding of arguments. For example, the structure

```
A + B * C - D / E
```

is the same as the structure

```
A + (B * C) - (D / E)
```

since '*' and '/' are defined to bind tighter than ' + ' and ' − '.

There are also several *built-in procedures* for comparing values of arithmetic expressions illustrated by the following dialogue:

```
?- 17 - 1 > 5 * 3.
   yes
?- 17 + 1 > 6 * 3.
   no
?- 5 >= 5.
   yes
?- 6 + 7 =:= 1 + 3 * 4.
   yes
?- 7 =:= 5 + 3.
   no
```

Note that all comparison predicates are built-in operators and may be written in infix notation. Like the operator 'is', they force the evaluation of their arguments, i.e. the computation of arithmetic expressions. At the time of the evaluation both arguments must be evaluable arithmetic expressions, i.e. all variables must already be instantiated to numbers.

An Overview of Built-in Operators

Besides the operator 'is' there are also several built-in operators for comparing numbers. These operators are *arithmetic procedures* whose arguments are evaluable arithmetic expressions.

X > Y	the value of X is greater than the value of Y
X < Y	the value of X is less than the value of Y
X > = Y	the value of X is greater than or equal to the value of Y
X = < Y	the value of X is less than or equal to the value of Y
X =:= Y	the values of X and Y are equal
X = \= Y	the values of X and Y are not equal

43

The built-in operators, used as functors that enable the construction of arithmetic expressions, are listed below. They have the following interpretation in the evaluation of arithmetic expressions:

X + Y	sum of X and Y
X − Y	difference of X and Y
X * Y	product of X and Y
X / Y	quotient of X and Y (for real division)
X div Y	quotient of X and Y (for integer division)
X mod Y	remainder of integer division of X by Y

Note

Like other Prolog structures, arithmetic expressions can also be represented in the form of a tree. The following three arithmetic expressions:

```
3*5
X*128 + 15/5
123*X + X/Y + 1212/(12+3)
```

can be written in the standard format for structures:

```
*(3,5)
+(*(X,128),/(15,5))
+(+(*(123,X),/(X,Y)),/(1212,+(12,3)))
```

and can be represented in the form of trees in Figure 3.7:

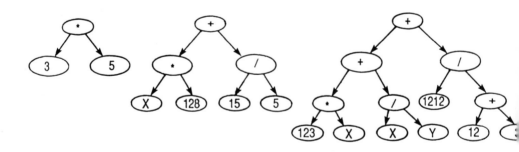

Figure 3.7 The tree representation of some arithmetic expressions.

Exercises

9. Suppose we have a procedure consisting of a set of facts in the form 'country(Name, Population, Area)'. Define a procedure 'density (Name, Density)'.

10. Let us have the rule:
```
p(X, Y) :-
    D is Y div X,
    Y is D * X.
```

What will Prolog answer to the following questions:
(a) ?- p(7, 21).
(b) ?- p(3, 10).
(c) ?- p(6, 30).
(d) ?- p(6, 35).
(e) ?- p(X, 21).
(f) (*) Can you simplify the above rule?

11. What will Prolog answer to the following questions:
(a) ?- X is 17 * 3 - 5.
(b) ?- 5 is X - 7.
(c) ?- 5 * 3 is 15.
(d) ?- 15 is 5 * 3.
(e) ?- 2 >= 2.
(f) ?- X is 5 * 3.
(g) ?- X =:= 5 * 3.
(h) ?- 17 - 3 =\= 6 * 4.

3.5 Summary

– Prolog data objects are called terms, which are either simple or compound. Compound terms are called structures.

– Simple terms are either constants or variables.

– Constants are either atoms or numbers and don't change their value during execution.

– Atoms are sequences of alphanumeric characters (including the underscore character '_') beginning with a lower-case letter, sequences of special characters or arbitrary sequences of characters enclosed in single quotes they stand for particular objects.

– Variables are sequences of alphanumeric characters (including the underscore character '_') beginning with an upper-case letter or an underscore and stand for unspecified individuals. They may change their value during execution.

– The anonymous variable '_' has an arbitrary value and cannot be shared.

– Structures consist of a functor name and a sequence of arguments enclosed in brackets. The former is an atom and the latter arbitrary Prolog terms. Structures stand for compound objects.

−A list is an ordered sequence of elements. Elements of a list may be arbitrary Prolog terms. A non-empty list consists of a head and a tail. An empty list ' [ ] ' has no head and no tail.

−A string is a list of ASCII codes. The built-in procedure 'name/2' is used to transform strings into atoms and vice versa.

−The operator ' = .. ' is a built-in procedure and is used to construct a structure on the left-hand side from the list on the right-hand side or vice versa. The functor of the structure corresponds to the head of the list and arguments to elements of the tail of the list.

−Arithmetic expressions are structures whose only functors are built-in arithmetic operators. They normally use the infix operator notation.

−The operator 'is' is a built-in procedure and is used to compute the value of the arithmetic expression at the right-hand side of the operator and to assign its value to the variable at the left-hand side, or it is used to compare it with a number at the left-hand side.

−The comparison operators '<', '>', '= <', '> =', '=:=' and '= \=' are built-in procedures that force the evaluation of arithmetic expressions on both sides and compare their values.

−Operators may be functors or predicates. Syntactically every predicate is a functor.

3.6 Solutions to Exercises

1.
(a) Ann hates Tom.
(b) '= = >' is a sign for implication.
(c) '&' is a sign for conjunction.
(d) '*' is a sign for anything.
(e) Someone can spend 10000 if his/her salary is greater than 10000.
(f) Tom can spend a certain amount of money if his salary is greater than this amount.
(g) Everybody hates everyone (including himself).
(h) Who hates whom?
(i) Whom does Ann hate?
(j) Does Ann hate someone?
(k) Does someone hate someone?
   (The answer will also be 'yes' if someone hates himself.)

2.
(a) ?- person(tom, Age, Address).
(b) ?- person(ann, Age, _).
(c) ?- person(Name, 10, _).
(d) ?- person(_, _, jamova_39).
(e) ?- person(Name, _, Address).
(f) ?- person(_, _, _).

3.
(a) flight(Flight_num, relation(From, To),
          departure(Day, time(Hour, Minute)))
(b) sentence(noun_phrase(determiner(a), noun(man)),
          verb_phrase(verb(watches),
                       noun_phrase(determiner(the),
                                    noun(match))))

4.

(a) X = sentence(pronoun(i), verb(love), pronoun(you))

(b) I = pronoun(i)
    Love = verb(love)
    You = pronoun(you)

(c) Who = tom
    Does = love
    Whom = you

5.

	Head	Tail
(a)	a	[b, c, d]
(b)	a	[b| X]
(c)	X	Y
(d)	X	[Y]
(e)	a	b
(f)	X	[ ]
(g)	unknown	unknown
(h)	[a, b, c| d]	[e, f, g| X]
(i)	does not exist	does not exist; Prolog answers 'no'
(j)	a	[b, c, d]

6.

(a) H = a
    T = [b,c]

(b) L = [a,b,c]

(c) H = a
    T = []

(d) L = [[a],a]

(e) H = []
    T = []

(f) H = a
    T = [c,d]

(g) L = [a|b]

(h) L = [a,b,c]
    T = [b,c]
    T1 = [c]

(i) no

7.

(a) third_element(X, [_, _, X | _]).

(b) last_element(X, [X]).
    last_element(X, [_,Tail]) :-
      last_element(X, Tail).
    /* This is a recursive definition. See section 5.1 */

47

8.

(a)
```
term( X) :- atomic( X).        % built-in procedure
term( X) :- var( X).           % built-in procedure
term( X) :-
    X =.. [ F | Terms],        % X is a structure
    length( Terms, N),         % see exercise 7 (b) in section 5.2
    function_symbol( F, N),
    terms( Terms).

terms( []).
terms( [ X| Terms]) :-         % This is a recursive
    term( X),                  % definition (see section 5.1)
    terms( Terms).
```

(b)
```
atomic_formula( X) :-
    X =.. [P | Terms],
    length( Terms, N),
    predicate( P, N),          % see exercise 7 (b) in section 5.2
    terms( Terms).             % See (a).
```

(c)
```
literal( A):-
    atomic_formula( A).        % See (b).
literal( not(A)):-
    atomic_formula( A).
```

9.
```
density( Country, Density) :-
    country( Country, Pop, Area),
    Density is Pop / Area.
```

10.
(a) yes
(b) no
(c) yes
(d) no
(e) the question will cause the execution error message
(f) p(X, Y) checks whether X is a divisor of Y. The rule can be simplified as follows:
```
p(X, Y) :- 0 is Y mod X.
```

11.
(a) X = 46
(b) the question will cause the execution error message
(c) no
(d) yes
(e) yes
(f) X = 15
(g) the question will cause the execution error message
(h) yes

48

Chapter 4

Execution and Meaning of Prolog Programs

The *declarative* meaning determines *what* a program does and the *procedural* meaning determines *how* this is done. In contrast with other programming languages, the programmer will be mostly concerned with the declarative aspect of programming, as the Prolog interpreter itself contains the deductive mechanism which "knows" how to execute the declarative definitions constituting a program.

4.1 Declarative and Procedural Meaning of Programs

When solving problems in Prolog we state properties and relations between objects that are unconditionally true (facts) and properties or relations that are true only under certain conditions (rules). When we ask Prolog questions, we specify what is to be done, without necessarily taking into consideration how Prolog actually works when trying to find solutions to the problem.

Consider the following program:

```
nice :-                 % Clause 1: It is nice if
   warm.                % it is warm.
nice :-                 % Clause 2: It is nice if
   sunny,               % it is sunny and
   not_windy.           % not windy.

warm :-                 % Clause 3: It is warm if
   temperature( T),     % the temperature is
   T > 20.              % greater than 20 degrees Celsius.

not_windy :-            % Clause 4: It is not windy if
   wind_speed( S),      % the wind speed is less than
   S < 5.               % 5 kilometers per hour.

sunny.                  % Clause 5.
temperature( 15).       % Clause 6.
wind_speed( 3).         % Clause 7.
```

49

The facts in the program state that it is sunny, that the temperature is 15 degrees Celsius and that the wind speed is 3 kilometres per hour. The rules determine under what conditions it is nice, warm and not windy. In order to define what is to be done, we have to ask Prolog a question for example: 'Is it nice?':

```
?- nice.
```

Of course the answer is 'yes'. Why? Simply because the second clause says that it is nice if it is sunny and not windy. We already know that it is sunny, so we must only prove that it is not windy. This follows from the fourth rule which states that it is not windy if the speed of the wind is less than 5 kilometres per hour, which we know to be the case. In fact, when proving whether a certain assertion is true, Prolog uses the same strategy.

In our example we have to prove that it is nice. We say that Prolog has to *satisfy* the goal 'nice' in the question. The system can prove that it is nice by the first or by the second rule. In our case, only the second rule can be successfully applied. We can read this rule as:

'To prove that it is nice, it must first be proved that it is sunny and then that it is not windy'
or
'To satisfy the goal 'nice' first satisfy the goal 'sunny' and then 'not__windy''.

These two interpretations are made according to the *procedural* meaning of the second rule, as opposed to its *declarative* meaning which is:

'It is nice if it is sunny and not windy'.

The goal 'sunny' is explicitly stated as a fact in the program so it is immediately satisfied. Namely, the procedural reading of the fact:

```
sunny.
```

is either

'It is proved that it is sunny'
or
'The goal 'sunny' is satisfied'

as opposed to the declarative reading which says,

'It is sunny'.

In order to prove the goal 'nice' we still have to satisfy the goal 'not__windy'. Reading the fourth clause in the procedural way we see that

'To satisfy the goal 'not__windy', we have to satisfy the goals 'wind__speed(S)' and 'S < 5''.

As we know from clause 7 (the fact stating that the wind speed is 3 kilometres per hour) these two goals are satisfied and thus the primary goal 'nice' is also satisfied.

In the example, we tried to point out the distinction between the declarative and the procedural meaning of a Prolog program. The declarative meaning is closer to our way of thinking and enables quicker programming as it, in fact, consists of defining the problem. On the other hand, the procedural meaning of a program determines how Prolog will satisfy goals. It is also concerned with the efficiency of execution and with the problem of *cycling*. This problem is illustrated in the following example. We could define that 'It is nice if it is nice', which can be stated by the following rule:

```
nice :- nice.
```

The declarative reading of this rule makes little sense, but doesn't seem harmful. However, the procedural reading

'To prove that it is nice we must prove that it is nice'

shows that the program will get into an infinite cycle, which cannot be handled by Prolog. Still, when programming in Prolog, a programmer may most of the time think in the declarative way.

Exercises

1. Consider the Prolog clauses from exercise 6, section 2.3. Translate the clauses into English by reading them in the procedural way.

2. (*) How will your interpretation of the clauses of exercise 1 change if we introduce the following questions:
(a) ?- boy(X).
(b) ?- husband(tom, Y).
(c) ?- lives(_).
(d) ?- transitory(happiness).
(Hint: first try to interpret questions in the declarative way!)

3. What is wrong with the following program?
```
parent( X, Y ) :-
   mother( X, Y );
   father( X, Y ).

mother( X, Y ) :-
   child( Y, X ),
   female( X ).

father( X, Y ) :-
   child( Y, X ),
   male( X ).

child( X, Y ) :-
   parent( Y, X ).
```

4.2 Matching

Consider again the program from the previous section concerned with answering the question:

```
?- nice.
```

Why can we prove that it is nice using the rule

```
nice :-
    sunny,
    not_windy.
```

but not with the rule

```
warm :-
    temperature( T),
    T > 20.
```

The obvious reason is that the head of the first rule is the literal 'nice', which *matches* the goal 'nice' in our question, and the head of the second rule is 'warm', which does not match the goal 'nice'.

For another example of matching, suppose we have the following facts:

```
temperature( 15).
wind_speed( 3).
```

The only goal in the question

```
?- temperature(X).
```

matches the first fact and can't match the second. In order to get the answer to a question, Prolog tries to match the goal with the head of some rule or with some fact. To do that it takes two terms and tries to make them identical. In the first example, the matching operation is simple as the two terms 'nice' and 'nice' are identical. In the second example, Prolog tries to make the terms 'temperature(15)' and 'temperature(X)' identical. The matching is completed by *instantiating* the variable X in the second term to the constant 15, and the answer to the question is:

```
X = 15
yes
```

If our question is:

```
?- temperature( 15).
```

Prolog answers 'yes' as the two terms (i.e. the two structures) to be matched are identical. But if we ask:

```
?- temperature(20).
```

the answer is 'no' as the constant 15 can not match the constant 20.

As another example, let us have the fact:

```
person( john, lennon).
```

If we ask:

```
?- person( Name).
```

Prolog will answer 'no' since this term, which is a structure with one argument, can not match a structure with two arguments. The appropriate question is:

```
?- person( Name, Fam_name).
Name = john
Fam_name = lennon
yes
```

A more formal definition of matching is that it takes two terms and tries to make them identical by instantiating the variables in both terms. Matching is performed according to the following rules:

(1) Two constants match if they are identical.
(2) An *uninstantiated variable* matches any term. Matching instantiates the variable to the term. If the term is also an uninstantiated variable the two variables become identical.
(3) Two structures match if they have a functor with the same name and arity, and if the corresponding arguments match according to one of these three rules.

If matching does not succeed, Prolog backtracks, but if successfully done, it produces the *most general* instantiation of variables. Examples in the sequel make this notion more understandable.

It is useful to represent structures with trees in order to understand why certain pairs of structures match and why others don't. Let us represent the structures 'a + b + c', 'X + Y + Z' and 'a + (b + c)' in Figure 4.1. The structures 'a + b + c' and 'X + Y + Z' match, but the structure 'a + (b + c)' doesn't match the other two structures.

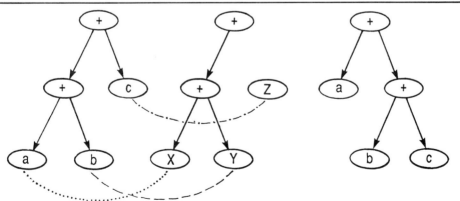

Figure 4.1   The tree representations of 'a + b + c', 'X + Y + Z' and 'a + (b + c)'. Arrows show how arguments of structures match.

53

The structure 'a + b * c' matches the structure 'X + Y' so that the variable X is instantiated to the constant a and Y is instantiated to the structure 'b * c'. The structure 'a + b * c' doesn't match the structure 'X * Y'. See the tree representation of these three structures in Figure 4.2.

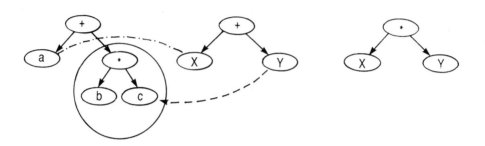

Figure 4.2 The tree representations of 'a + b * c', 'X + Y' and 'X * Y'. Arrows show how arguments of structures match.

We can ask Prolog whether two terms match by using the built-in operator ' = ' and we may have the following dialogue where ' = ' is used as a request for matching:

```
?- a + b + c = X + Y + Z.
X = a
Y = b
Z = c
yes
?- a + b + c = A + (B + C).
no
?- a + b * c = X + Y.
X = a
Y = b * c
yes
?- a + b * c = X * Y.
no
?- X = 5.
X = 5
yes
?- X = 2 + 3.
X = 2 + 3
yes
?- a + b = a + b.
yes
?- a + b = b + a.
no
?- [ X, Y, Z] = [ 1, 2, 3].
X = 1
Y = 2
Z = 3
yes
```

```
?- [ X | Y] = [ one, two, three].    % See the two structures
X = one                              % in Figure 4.3.
Y = [ two, three]
yes
?- [ X| Y] = [a].                    % See the two structures
X = a                                % in Figure 4.3.
Y = []
yes
?- [ _| _] = [].                     % a structure does not
no                                   % match an atom
```

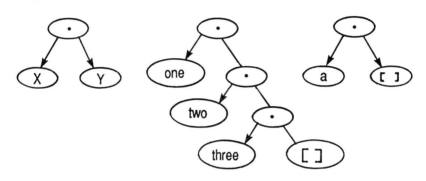

Figure 4.3   The tree representation of structures '[X| Y]', '[one, two, three]' and '[a]'.

Now consider two more complex structures, both representing a triangle defined by three points: 'triangle(p(1,Y), p(X,Y), T3)' and 'triangle(T1, p(2,3), p(2,2))'. The tree forms of these structures are given in Figure 4.4.

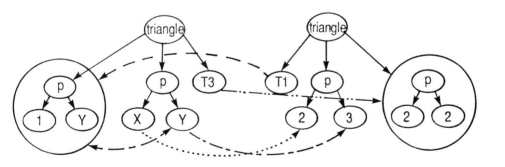

Figure 4.4   The tree representations of 'triangle(p(1,Y), p(X,Y), T3)' and 'triangle(T1, p(2,3), p(2,2))'. Arrows show how arguments of structures match.

The matching process starts at the root of the tree and finds out that the two functors 'triangle' match. Then the corresponding arguments are matched

```
p(1,Y) = T1
p(X,Y) = p(2,3)
T3 = p(2,2)
```

and variables are instantiated to:

```
X = 2
Y = 3
T1 = p(1,3)
T3 = p(2,2)
```

Note that the variable Y appears twice in the first structure. When Y is instantiated to 3, the value of T1 becomes p(1,3).

Let us try to match the structures 'triangle(p(1,Y), p(X,Y), T3)' and 'triangle(T1, p(2,3), p(W,2))', which differ from the above example only in the third argument of the second structure. In this case the matching process does not instantiate all variables to constants. The variable T3 is instantiated to 'p(W,2)' where W remains an uninstantiated variable.

We say that matching results in the most general instantiation of variables that still suffices for both structures to become identical. Obviously, the variable W could be instantiated to any constant and the two structures would still be identical, but such instantiation would not be the most general one.

Different Types of Equality

We have already seen that equality in Prolog can be interpreted in various ways. We may ask whether the values of two arithmetic expressions are equal, using the operator ' =:= ' and want to match a variable or a number with the value of an arithmetic expression using the operator 'is'. A third kind of equality is defined by the operator ' = ' which checks whether two structures match and finds the most general instantiation of variables.

Still another kind of equality is defined by the operator ' == ', which enables us to check whether two terms are literally identical without matching them. The use of the operator ' == ' is illustrated by the following dialogue:

```
?- a + b == a + b.
yes
?- X + Y == a + b.
no
?- X == Y.
no
?- X == X.
yes
?- a + b = X, X == a + b.
yes
```

The following is a complete set of equality operators and their negations:

X = Y	X is equal to Y, if X and Y match (for arbitrary terms X and Y)
X == Y	X is literaly equal to Y, if X and Y are identical (for arbitrary terms X and Y)
X \== Y	X is not literaly equal to Y (for arbitrary terms X and Y)
X =:= Y	the value of X equals the value of Y (for arithmetic expressions X and Y)
X =\= Y	the value of X is not equal to the value of Y (for arithmetic expressions X and Y)
X is Y	X is Y, if X matches the value of Y (where X is a variable or a constant and Y is an arithmetic expression)

Notes

1. Consider the answer to the following question:

```
?- X = f( X).
X = f( f( f( f( f( f( f( ......
```

A variable will match a structure in which it appears, although this is not correct. For efficiency reasons most Prolog implementations do not check for occurences of a variable in a structure that is to be matched with this same variable. When matching, we get a loop (see Figure 4.5). This problem is referred to as the *occurs check* problem, but we will not look at it in detail here. It also represents the only difference between *unification* in logic and matching in Prolog.

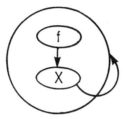

Figure 4.5   X matches the structure 'f(X)'.

2. When a variable is uninstantiated or partially instantiated it represents an object that is not completely specified. When it is instantiated, it denotes one particular object. An example of a stepwise instantiation of a variable is:

```
?- X = Y + a, Y = Z + b, Z = W + c, W = e + d.
X = e + d + c + b + a
Y = e + d + c + b
Z = e + d + c '
W = e + d
yes
```

This is very useful for dealing with unbounded structures. Note that a similar technique was proposed for handling unbounded lists in Note 3 of section 3.3.

Exercises

4. How do the following pairs of structures match:
(a) date(Day, Month, 1983) and date(D, june, Y)
(b) triangle(p(1,1), A, p(2,3)) and triangle(X, p(4,Y), p(2,Y))
(c) X and [a, b, c]
(d) [a, b| X] and [a, b, c]
(e) [a, X, Y] and [a, f(b), c]
(f) [X| [Y]] and [1, 2, 3]
(g) [X, Y] and [1, 2, 3]
(h) [X, Y] and [a, [b, c]]
(i) [a, b, c| X] and [a, b, c]
(j) [X| Y] and [a]

(k) [X| Y] and [ ]
(l) [X, Y, Z] and [a| [b| [c]]]
(m) (*) [X, Y, Z] and [a, b| c]
(n) (*) [2| X] and X
(o) (*) [X| Y] and X

5. What will Prolog answer to the following questions:
(a) ?- X = 1 + 2.
(b) ?- X is 1 + 2.
(c) ?- X =:= 1 + 2.
(d) ?- X == 1 + 2.
(e) ?- X = 1 + 2, X == 1 + 2.
(f) ?- 1 + 2 = 2 + 1.
(g) ?- 1 + 2 =:= 2 + 1.
(h) (*) ?- X = 1 + 2, Y is X.
(i) (*) ?- X = 1 + 2, Y is X * 3.
(j) (*) ?- X = 1 + 2, X * 3 = 1 + 2 * 3.
(k) (**) ?- (X + Y) + Z = A + (B + C).
(l) (**) ?- X = a + Y, Y = b + Z, Z = c + d.

6. A program consists of four facts:
```
loves( jane, tom).
loves( ann, mark).
loves( tom, jane).
loves( tom, ann).
```

How will Prolog answer the following questions:
(a) ?- loves(X, tom).
(b) ?- loves(ann, X).
(c) ?- loves(X, Y), loves(Y, ann).
(d) ?- loves(X, Y), loves(Y, X).
(e) (*) ?- loves(X, Y), loves(Y, Z), loves(Z, W),
    loves(W, X).

7. (*) Consider the program consisting of only one clause: 'concat(X-Y, Y-Z, X-Z).'
What will Prolog answer to the following questions:
(a) ?- concat([a, b, c| X]-X, [d, e| Y]-Y, Z).
(b) ?- concat([a| X]-X, Y, [a, b, c, d, e| Z]-Z).
(c) ?- concat([1, 2| X]-X, [3, 4| Y]-Y, Z),
        concat(Z, [5| W]-W, R).

8. Define the relation 'empty(List)' which is true if the list List is empty.

9. (*) What is wrong with the following rule:
```
brother( X, Y) :-
    parent( Z, X),
    parent( Z, Y),
    male( X).
```

10. Figure 2.1 of exercise 2, Chapter 2 shows a tree that represents relations in school. Define a relation 'colleague(X, Y)' which states that X and Y are colleagues if they have the same head or the same teacher.

11. (**) Express in Prolog the following statement that leads to an infinite regress: 'If you have a goal you will have to find a path to achieve that goal, which is your new goal'.

4.3 Execution of Prolog Programs

Let us see how Prolog executes the program given in section 4.1:

```
nice :-                        % Clause 1.
    warm.
nice :-                        % Clause 2.
    sunny,
    not_windy.

warm :-                        % Clause 3.
    temperature( T),
    T > 20.

not_windy :-                   % Clause 4.
    wind_speed( S),
    S < 5.

sunny.                         % Clause 5.
temperature( 15).              % Clause 6.
wind_speed( 3).                % Clause 7.
```

In section 4.1 we mentioned only the strategy which Prolog uses to find a solution to the given problem. Here, we follow the execution of the program step by step and illustrate the trace of execution in Figure 4.6.

(1) When we ask Prolog the question:

```
?- nice.
```

'nice' becomes the goal to be satisfied. In order to satisfy the goal, Prolog searches the program in *top-down* manner trying to find a clause whose head matches the goal. The first clause that matches the goal 'nice' is the rule:

```
nice :-
    warm.
```

Prolog makes a *variant* of this clause and matches the goal with the head of a variant (a variant of a clause is a clause with new, renamed variables in order to make it independent of the original one to prevent changes of the program).

(2) Now 'warm' becomes the goal to be satisfied. Prolog again searches the program top-down to find a clause whose head matches the goal 'warm'. It finds the rule:

```
warm :-
    temperature( T),
    T > 20.
```

Prolog matches the goal with the head (of a variant) of this rule.

(3) Now there are two goals in the body of the rule to be satisfied: 'temperature (T)' and 'T > 20'. Prolog attempts to satisfy the goals in the body from *left to right*, starting with the left-most goal. When trying to match the goal 'temperature (T)' it finds the fact:

```
temperature( 15).
```

which matches the goal. The variable T gets instantiated to 15. Since a fact has an empty body, there are no new goals to be added to the list of goals to be satisfied.

(4) The only goal that has to be satisfied is now 'T > 20'. Since the variable T is instantiated to 15, Prolog tries to satisfy the goal:

```
15 > 20
```

'>/2' is a built-in procedure, so Prolog need not search the program for its definition. Since 15 is less than 20, Prolog can not satisfy this goal. The goal *fails* and Prolog *automatically backtracks* to the last goal that was matched, i.e. it backtracks to the goal 'temperature(T)' and tries to match this goal in another way. While backtracking, the variable T gets uninstantiated. By backtracking Prolog returns to the last successfully matched goal and tries to satisfy it in a different way.

(5) To satisfy the goal 'temperature(T)', Prolog doesn't search the program from the beginning, but continues from the clause where this goal was matched last. It now starts with the fact 'temperature(15)' and searches down to the end of the program for another clause whose head could match the goal 'temperature(T)'. Since there is no other clause in the program whose head matches the goal 'temperature(T)', it fails.

(6) Prolog again automatically backtracks to the last goal that was successfully matched, i.e to the goal 'warm'. Now it tries to find an alternative clause whose head would match the goal 'warm'. Note again that in order to match this goal Prolog does not search from the beginning of the program. The search continues from the clause where the goal was previously matched. A search for another clause whose head can match the goal 'warm' is unsuccessful, so Prolog backtracks to the goal 'nice'.

(7) Prolog now finds the second clause as a new matching rule.

```
nice :-
    sunny,
    not_windy.
```

(8) The execution now runs similarly as above. The goals to be satisfied are now 'sunny' and 'not__windy'. The goal 'sunny' is satisfied by matching it with the fact

```
sunny.
```

(9) The goal 'not__windy' is matched with the head of the rule

```
not_windy :-
  wind_speed( S),
  S < 5.
```

(10) The two goals to be satisfied are now 'wind__speed(S)' and 'S < 5'. The first goal is satisfied by matching it with the fact

```
wind_speed( 3).
```

and instantiating the variable S to 3.

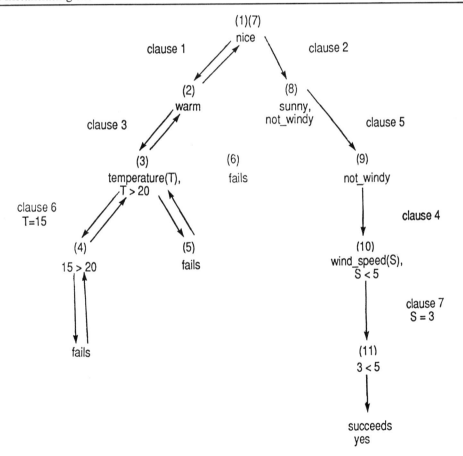

Figure 4.6 The execution trace of the goal 'nice'. The left branch fails to satisfy the goal while the right branch succeeds. The numbers in brackets denote particular execution steps explained in the text.

(11) The last goal to be satisfied is '3 < 5', which, of course, succeeds. As there are no more goals to be satisfied, the goal in the original question is satisfied and Prolog answers 'yes'.

Rules of Execution

The execution of Prolog programs is performed according to the following rules:

(1) Put all the goals from the question into a list of goals to be satisfied.
(2) If there are no more goals in the list of goals to be satisfied then the goals in the question are satisfied and the execution stops, else take the left-most goal from the list of goals and search the program in a top-down manner until a clause whose head matches the goal is found.
(3) If such a clause exists, then make a variant of the clause, match the head of the variant with the goal and put the goals from the body of the variant at the beginning of the list of goals to be satisfied. Go to (2).
(4) If such a clause does not exist, then uninstantiate all the variables that got instantiated in the last matching, return to the last successfully matched goal and search for another clause whose head matches the goal and go to (3). The search for such a clause is performed downwards from the clause that previously matched the goal. If there was no previously matched goal then the goals in question can not be satisfied and the execution stops.

We can see from Figure 4.6 that the execution of Prolog programs can be viewed as searching the tree of all possible execution paths. Prolog searches the tree in a *depth-first left-to-right* manner. When it reaches the end of a branch, it automatically backtracks to the first branching node above.

We say that the execution of Prolog programs is *non-deterministic* because of multiple execution paths. Of course, if all procedures in a program consisted of only one clause, then only one execution path would exist.

Obtaining Alternative Solutions

Consider the program consisting of two facts:

```
knowledgeable( aristotle).
knowledgeable( einstein).
```

If we ask Prolog a question that contains a variable, it will give us its instantiation:

```
?- knowledgeable( X).
X = aristotle
```

The fact 'knowledgeable(aristotle)' is namely the first fact in the program. We may now want to get alternative answers to the question. We can force Prolog to find another solution by typing in a semicolon ';', which invokes backtracking. Prolog continues execution by failing the last goal that was satisfied and by backtracking as in normal execution in order to find another clause whose head matches that goal. The whole dialogue is then the following:

```
?- knowledgeable( X).
X = aristotle;
X = einstein;
no
```

After all solutions are displayed, Prolog answers 'no' as there are no other knowledgeable persons (in the program, of course).

Notes

1. In the above example we met an important feature of Prolog. Prolog assumes that everything that can be derived from the program is true and everything else is not true. For example, if we ask Prolog whether a dog is an animal:

```
?- animal( dog).
```

and such fact is not a part of the program nor can be derived from it, Prolog will answer 'no', although it can not know whether it is true or not. The described feature is referred to as the *closed-world assumption*. This is an important feature to be considered when programming in Prolog. It will be further considered in section 4.4 when dealing with negation.

2. We have already seen that a Prolog program may be viewed as a knowledge base of a particular problem domain. Another way of interpreting a Prolog program is as a set of axioms (in the form of facts and rules) from which we can prove theorems (get answers to questions) using logical deductive reasoning. We state a theorem (we ask a question) and Prolog tries to prove it (derive it) from the given axioms (program). The Prolog interpreter can thus be seen as a theorem prover. This view is illustrated in Figure 4.7.

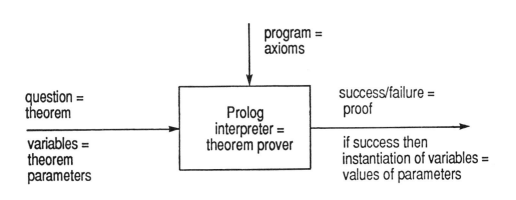

Figure 4.7 The Prolog interpreter as a theorem prover.

3. In section 4.1 we saw that from a declarative point of view the rule:

```
nice :-
    nice.
```

is correct, but it leads to an infinite loop according to the procedural reading of the program. What will happen if we ask Prolog the question:

```
?- nice.
```

Prolog tries to satisfy the goal by matching it with the head of a rule. The new goal to be satisfied is again the goal 'nice', since it is the only goal in the body of the rule. So Prolog will keep on looping and will not terminate as long as there is still enough memory available for execution.

A less obvious example of a cyclic definition is the program

```
parent( X, Y) :- child( Y, X).
...
child( X, Y) :- parent( Y, X).
```

Logically the two rules are correct, but the execution will end in an infinite loop similar to the one in the previous example. This is analoguous to a definition in a dictionary:

precedence – see priority
...
priority – see precedence

which is obviously not very useful and ends in an infinite loop in the case of a senseless reader (as in the case of a stupid computer).

When programming in Prolog we should pay attention to such procedural peculiarities. We should consider also the procedural meaning of programs and not only their declarative correctness.

Exercises

12. In which clauses (rules) of the 'weather' program may we reverse the order of goals in the body?

13. Assume we have the procedure:

```
d( [], 0).
d( [ X| L], s( D)) :- d( L, D).
```

What will be the answer to the following questions:

(a) ?- d([1, 2, 3, 4], X).
(b) ?- d(L, s(s(s(0)))).

14. Let us have the procedure:
```
inv( X + Y, Y1 + X1) :- inv( X, X1), inv( Y, Y1).
inv( X, X).
```
Find all answers to the question:
```
?- inv( 1 + ( 2 + 3), Z).
```

15. (*) Here are two procedures for searching an element of a list:
```
member1( X, [ X| _]).
member1( X, [ _| Tail]) :-
  member1( X, Tail).


member2( X, [ _| Tail) :-
  member2( X, Tail).
member2( X, [ X| _]).
```

Draw the execution trace, simulating the execution of both procedures when answering the questions:
(a) ?- member1(2, [1, 2, 3, 4]).
(b) ?- member2(2, [1, 2, 3, 4]).
(c) Which procedure is better?

16. Powdered milk is issued from the hotel storage if there is no fresh milk in stock. Part of the procedure for this is the following:

```
issue( milk, Litres, fresh, Litres) :-
  stock( milk, fresh, L),
  L >= Litres,
  issued( milk, fresh, Litres).   % Updates the stock evidence.
issue( milk, Litres, powdered, Kilos) :-
  Kilos is Litres * 0.125,
  issued( milk, powdered, Kilos).
% One litre of milk corresponds to 0.125 kilos of powdered
% milk.
```

What would happen if we changed the order of clauses in the procedure?

17. We have the following procedure for computing the greater number of two given numbers:
```
max( X, Y, X) :- X >= Y.
max( X, Y, Y).
```
What will Prolog answer to the following questions:
(a) ?- max(15, 13, X).
(b) ?- max(15, 13, X), 2 * X < 30.
(c) Write a correct program for 'max'.

18. Are the following two questions procedurally equivalent?
```
?- f1( X), f2( Y), X = Y, X == Y.
?- f1( X), f2( Y), X == Y, X = Y.
```

65

4.4 Negation as Failure

Until now we have been dealing with goals that have to be satisfied to become *true*. In the 'weather' program from section 4.1 we had the rule:

```
nice :-
  sunny,
  not_windy.
```

which can be interpreted as: 'we can conclude that it is 'nice' if it is true that it is 'sunny' and 'not_windy''. We may also have a slightly different interpretation: 'we can conclude that it is 'nice' if it is true that it is 'sunny' and if it is *not true* that it is 'windy''. We now have the goal 'windy' that must not be satisfied if we want to conclude that 'nice' is true. We now have to define, when it is windy, for example, by the rule:

```
windy :-
  wind_speed( S),
  S >= 5.
```

According to the second interpretation of the rule which defines when it is nice, we may rewrite it as:

```
nice :-
  sunny,
  not (windy).
```

We used the built-in procedure *not* with one argument. The goal 'not(windy)' succeeds if the goal 'windy' fails and vice versa. In our program we had a fact:

```
wind_speed( 3).
```

therefore the goal 'windy' is not satisfied and the goal 'not(windy)' is. Since the negated goal must fail if the negation is to be satisfied, Prolog negation is referred to as *negation as failure*.

Let us now extend the 'weather' program. We may define that it is cold if the temperature is less than 0 degrees Celsius and that it is hot if the temperature is greater than 30 degrees, i.e.

```
cold :- temperature( T),
  T < 0.

hot :- temperature( T),
  T > 30.
```

We can now define the state 'nice' with more conditions:

```
nice :-
  sunny,
  not((windy, cold; hot)).
```

In this case, the argument of the predicate 'not/1' is the logical combination of goals, enclosed in brackets. As previously shown, Prolog tries to satisfy goals which constitute the argument of the 'not' procedure. If this succeeds, the negation of the goal fails and vice versa. In our case, we have the fact 'temperature(15)', therefore the negation succeeds.

Let us now consider a program which describes a hierarchy in a group of strip-cartoon heroes with a set of facts.

```
chief( no_1, grunf).
chief( no_1, clodovik).
chief( no_1, chief).
chief( grunf, noser).
chief( chief, rock).
chief( chief, ford).
chief(chief,jeremy).
```

The hierarchy is shown in Figure 4.8.

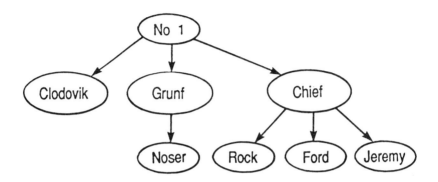

Figure 4.8   The hierarchy in a group of strip-cartoon heroes.

Our task is to define the procedure 'head(X)' where the goal 'head(X)' is true if X is someone's chief and has no superior chief. The procedure is defined by the rule:

```
head( X) :-
    chief( X, _),
    not( chief(_, X)).
```

In this example, the argument of the predicate 'not/1' contains variables. As stated above, the goal 'not(chief(_, X))' succeeds if the goal 'chief(_, X)' fails. If we ask Prolog the question:

```
?- head( X).
```

the only possible answer is

```
X = no_1
```

As there is no fact which would match the goal 'chief(_, no_1)', the goal 'not(chief(_, no_1))' succeeds. But what would happen if we reversed the goals in the body?

```
head( X) :-
    not( chief( _, X)),
    chief( X, _).
```

Logically both rules are equivalent, but if we now ask

```
?- head( X).
```

Prolog answers 'no', and if we ask

```
?- head( no_1).
```

Prolog answers 'yes'. At first glance the rule seems correct but when Prolog tries to answer the question '?- head(X)' by trying to satisfy the goal 'chief(__, X)', the variable X is not yet instantiated. Prolog now finds such a value of X for which the goal is satisfied (for example X = grunf). Therefore the goal 'not(chief(__, X))' does not succeed. On the other hand, when asking '?- head(no__1)' the variable X in the goal 'chief(__, X)' becomes instantiated to 'no__1' and 'not(chief(__, X))' succeeds.

This example shows that negation in Prolog is procedurally defined and is not equivalent to negation in logic. You should be aware that the procedure 'not' implements negation as the failure of proving that the goal is true.

Notes

1. The procedure 'not' can not instantiate any variable since it succeeds only if the argument goals fail. As an example we may state a naive definition of a person with no children:

```
has_no_children( X) :-
   not( child( _, X)).
```

The procedure will give correct answers only if in a question X is already instantiated.

2. Prolog assumes that everything that is stated in the program or that can be derived from it is true and everything else is false. We have referred to this as the 'closed world assumption' in the previous section. Therefore the answer to the question:

```
?- not( clever( user)).
```

is 'yes' although we (and the program) know nothing about the user.

3. We have already met some built-in procedures implementing negation, namely:

```
X \== Y is the negation of X == Y
X =\= Y is the negation of X =:= Y
X < Y   is the negation of X >= Y
X > Y   is the negation of X =< Y
```

Exercises

19. Define a procedure 'most__general(Class)' by using the goal 'subclass(X, Y)' that is satisfied if X is a subclass of Y.

20. Are the following pairs of questions equivalent:
(a) '?- not(not(sunny)).' and '?- sunny.'
(b) '?- not(not(parent(ann, tom))).' and '?- parent(ann, tom).'
(c) '?- not(not(clever(X))).' and '?- clever(X).'

(d) '?- not(not(X = 2 + 3)).' and '?- X = 2 + 3.'
(e) '?- not(X + Y == 2 + 3).' and '?- X + Y \== 2 + 3.'
(f) '?- not(X + Y = 2 + 3).' and '?- X + Y \== 2 + 3.'

21. Let us have the procedure 'prime(X)' which checks whether X is a prime number. Can you define a procedure 'not_a_prime(X)' using only the goal 'prime(X)' and the procedure 'not'?

22. In section 4.3, exercise 16 we had a procedure for issuing milk from a hotel storage 'issue(milk, Quantity, Type, Issued)'. Try to correct the clauses of the procedure to be declaratively correct in order to allow the sequence of clauses to be reversed.

23. In section 2.5 we had a program for determining the acceptability of a car. Change the program so that the categories 'very_good' and 'good' become disjoint, i.e. that the cars which are 'very_good' are not also 'good'.

24. (**) Translate the following questions into Prolog (Hint: Suppose facts are given in the form
'person(P)', 'likes (p,wine)', 'play (P,I)':
(a) Is it true that nobody likes wine?
(b) Does everybody like wine?
(c) Does anybody play all instruments?
(d) Does everybody play some instrument?
(e) Does everybody play all instruments?

4.5 Different Use of Procedures

Assume we have the procedure implementing a personal telephone directory:

```
tel( rudi, 0273-606755).
tel( judith, 041-5526400).
tel( carl, 217-3331376).
```

To get Carl's number we form a question:

```
?- tel( carl, N).
N = 217-3331376
yes
```

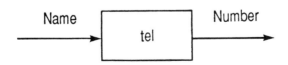

Figure 4.9 Procedure 'tel' where Name is an input and Number is an output argument.

This is the standard way of using the procedure. We say that 'carl' is an *input* argument and N is an *output* argument of a procedure. The procedure 'tel' can be seen as a box on Figure 4.9.

But this is not the only possible way of using the procedure. We may want to check whether someone's number is correct:

```
?- tel( rudi, 0273-606755).
yes
```

or we may want to find out whose telephone number is the one we have in mind:

```
?- tel( Name, 041-5526400).
Name = judith
yes
```

We may also simply want to display the entire list of our friends' telephone numbers:

```
?- tel( Name, Num).
Name = rudi
Num = 0273-606755;
Name = judith
Num = 041-5526400;
Name = carl
Num = 217-3331376;
no
```

Both arguments of the procedure 'tel' may be used as input or as output arguments. There are four possible ways of using the procedure 'tel'. One was represented in Figure 4.9 and the other three ways are represented in Figure 4.10.

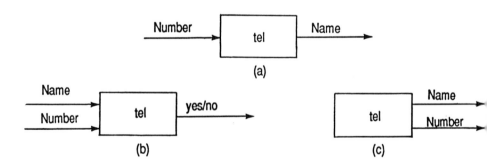

Figure 4.10 Procedure 'tel' where (a) Number is the input argument and Name is the output argument, (b) both Name and Number are input arguments and (c) both Name and Number are output arguments.

Most Prolog procedures can be used in several different ways. This is not the case in other programming languages where procedures can be used only in one direction, with predefined input and output arguments. Actually, some Prolog procedures may be used in only one direction, due to the Prolog procedural peculiarities. Let us consider some that we have already met.

Arithmetic computations using the operator 'is' can not be used in the reverse way. If we ask:

```
?- X is 2 + 18 / 5.
```

we get the result X = 5.6, but if we asked:

```
?- 5.6 is A + B / C.
```

Prolog would have to find all triples (A, B, C) such that the expression 'A + B / C' would give the result 5.6. In such case the error message is usually displayed.

It might seem that the operator ' = ' enables the reversed direction of computation in arithmetic. We already know that this is not the case as this operator is used to match the structures and not to force the computation of arithmetic expressions. For example:

```
?- X = 2 + 18 / 5.
X = 2 + 18 / 5
yes
?- A + B / C = 2 + 18 / 5.
A = 2
B = 18
C = 5
yes
?- 3 = 2 + 1.
no
?- 2 + 1 = 2 + 1.
yes
```

Therefore when thinking of how the input and output arguments can be used in procedures that include arithmetic computations, we must take into account how Prolog actually executes them. Obviously, the following procedure can not be used in the reversed direction:

```
convert( Kilometres, Miles) :-
    Miles is Kilometres / 1.609.
```

and in the procedure:

```
higher( X, Y) :-
    high( X, Hx),
    high( Y, Hy),
    Hx > Hy.
```

we must not change the order of goals in the body since Hx and Hy must be already instantiated if the goal 'Hx > Hy' is to be satisfied.

71

The use of the predicate 'not' also prevents using procedures in different ways. We can use the procedure:

```
has_no_children( X ) :-
    not( child( _, X)).
```

only to check whether a certain person has no children but we can not use it to find out who are the persons that have no children. As there is usually some person X that has a child, the goal 'child(_, X)' succeeds and the goal 'not(child(_, X))' fails. To overcome this problem, we can introduce an additional condition which will force X to be instantiated before executing the goal 'not(child(_, X))':

```
has_no_children( X ) :-
    person( X ),
    not( child( _, X)).
```

Note that the order of goals in the body of the above rule must not be reversed.

Exercises

25. Correct the following rule so that it can be used in several different ways:
```
aunt( X, Y ) :-
    parent( Z, Y ),
    Z \== X,
    parent( G, Z ),
    parent( G, X ),
    female( X ).
```

26. (*) Metalogical procedures 'var/1', 'nonvar/1', 'number/1' and 'atom/1' can be used to find out if a given term is a variable, not a variable, a number, and an atom, respectively. Define the procedure 'X iss Y' that will perform as 'is/2' except that it will not cause the execution error message if Y is not completely instantiated to numbers but will simply fail.

27. Define the procedure 'convert(Kilometres, Miles)' which will work if at least one argument is instantiated. (Hint: use the procedure 'iss/2' from exercise 26.)

28. Can you define the procedure 'sum' determining a relation between the arguments X, Y, Z so that sum(X, Y, Z) is true if Z is the sum of X and Y, and that will work if at least two arguments are instantiated? (Hint: use the procedure 'iss/2' from exercise 26.)

29. What is wrong with the following definition of the operator '\==':
```
X \== Y :- not( X = Y).
```

4.6 Summary

–The declarative meaning of Prolog programs is concerned with what relations are defined in the program. The procedural meaning determines how the result is obtained.

– A Prolog programmer can concentrate on the declarative way of thinking and may leave most of the procedural details to the Prolog interpreter. This approach makes programming easier and more efficient than in procedural languages.

– The procedural aspects of programming must be considered in order to avoid deficiencies of the interpreter as is the danger of cycling, to appropriately order the clauses in a program and goals in the body of a clause, and to use input and output arguments of procedures correctly. In large programs, one must also consider procedural aspects in order to ensure the efficiency of execution.

– A variable matches any Prolog term and is instantiated to that term.

– Two structures match if they have the same functor and arity and if their corresponding arguments match.

– Questions force the execution of Prolog programs. Prolog tries to satisfy goals in a question from left to right.

– Prolog tries to satisfy a goal by matching it with the head of a clause and further by trying to satisfy goals in the body of that clause. In order to find a matching clause, Prolog searches a program in top-down manner.

– If a goal can not be satisfied, Prolog automatically backtracks to the last goal that was successfully matched and tries to match it with the head of some other clause. When searching for such a clause, Prolog continues searching from the clause with which the goal was previously matched. When backtacking, variables are uninstantiated, i.e. loose the values they acquired in the last match.

– Prolog assumes that everything is stated in the program or can be derived from the program. This property is referred to as the 'closed world assumption'.

– Negation in Prolog succeeds if the negated goal fails. This is referred to as negation as failure. Negation in Prolog can not instantiate any variable in the negated goal.

– Most Prolog procedures can be used in several different ways. The exceptions are procedures using arithmetic operations and negation of goals that contain uninstantiated variables.

4.7 Solutions to Exercises

1.
(a) To prove that X is a boy, prove that X is a child and that X is male.
(b) To prove that X is a husband of Y prove that X is married to Y and that X is male.
(c) To prove that X lives prove that X is born, that X grows and that X multiplies.
(d) It is proved that everything is transitory.

2. Note that the interpretation of questions is written in brackets.
(a) (Is it true that X is a boy?) or (Who is a boy?) To find such X that is a boy, find an X that is a child and that is male.

(b) (Is it true that Tom is a husband of Y?) or (Whose husband is Tom?) To find a Y such that Tom is a husband of Y, find a Y such that Tom is her husband provided that Tom is male.
(c) (Is there anyone/anything that lives?) To prove that there is something that lives, find something that was born, that grows and that multiplies.
(d) (Is happiness transitory?) It is proved that hapiness is transitory.

3. From the declarative point of view the program is correct, although in the procedural sense it is wrong as it includes a cycle: 'parent/2' is defined by 'father/2' and 'mother/2'; 'father/2' and 'mother/2' are defined by 'child/2'; 'child/2' is again defined by 'parent/2'.

4.
(a) Day = D, Month = june, Y = 1983
(b) X = p(1,1), A = p(4,3), Y = 3
(c) X = [a, b, c]
(d) X = [c]
(e) X = f(b), Y = c
(f) do not match
(g) do not match
(h) X = a, Y = [b, c]
(i) X = []
(j) X = a, Y = []
(k) do not match
(l) X = a, Y = b, Z = c
(m) do not match
(n) X = [2| 2| 2| 2| 2| 2| ....
(o) X = [[[[[[[[[....

5.
(a) X = 1 + 2
(b) X = 3
(c) execution error message is displayed
(d) no
(e) X = 1 + 2
(f) no
(g) yes
(h) X = 1 + 2
    Y = 3
(i) X = 1 + 2
    Y = 9   % Y is (1 + 2) * 3
(j) no   % (1 + 2) * 3 doesn't match 1 + (2 * 3)
(k) A = X + Y
    Z = B + C
(l) X = a + (b + (c + d))
    Y = b + (c + d)
    Z = c + d

6.
(a) X = jane
(b) X = mark
(c) X = jane
    Y = tom
(d) X = jane
    Y = tom
(e) X = jane
    Y = tom
    Z = jane
    W = tom

7.
(a) X = [d, e| Y]
    Z = [a, b, c, d, e| Y]-Y
(b) X = [b, c, d, e| Z]
    Y = [b, c, d, e| Z]-Z
(c) X = [3, 4, 5| W]
    Y = [5| W]
    Z = [1, 2, 3, 4, 5| W]-[5| W]
    R = [1, 2, 3, 4, 5| W]-W
    /* This notation enables efficient implementation of the
       concatenation of two lists. This technique is explained in
       section 6.4. */

8. empty ([]).

9. The goal 'X \ = = Y' is missing in the condition part of the rule. Without this additional goal, the question
    ?- brother(tom, tom).
would succeed, which should not happen.

10.
    colleague(X, Y) :-
      teacher(Z, X),
      teacher(Z, Y),
      X \== Y.
    colleague(X, Y) :-
      head(Z, X),
      head(Z, Y),
      X \== Y.

11.
    find(Goal) :- Goal = path_to(Goal).
The question
    ?- find(Goal).
would lead to the infinite output
    Goal = path_to(path_to(path_to(path_to(...

12. We may reverse the order of goals only in the second clause.

13.
(a) X = s(s(s(s(0))))
(b) L = [A, B, C]
    % or L = [_1, _2, _3] or any three different variables
    % chosen by the Prolog interpreter.

14.
  Z = 3 + 2 + 1; Z = 2 + 3 + 1; Z = 1 + (2 + 3); no

15.
(a) See Figure 4.11.

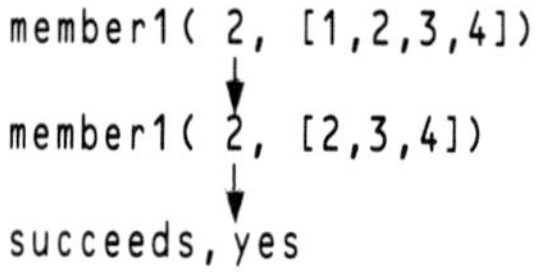

```
member1( 2, [1,2,3,4])
        ↓
member1( 2, [2,3,4])
        ↓
succeeds, yes
```

Figure 4.11   The execution trace.

(b) See Figure 4.12.

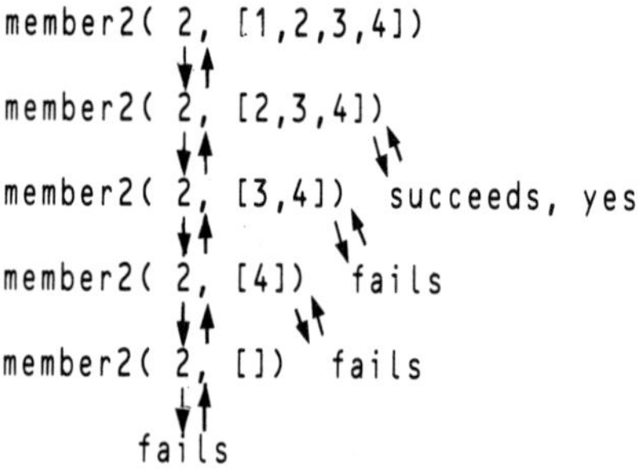

```
member2( 2, [1,2,3,4])
        ↓↑
member2( 2, [2,3,4])
        ↓↑            ↖↑
member2( 2, [3,4])   succeeds, yes
        ↓↑         ↖↑
member2( 2, [4])    fails
        ↓↑       ↖↑
member2( 2, [])    fails
        ↓↑↑
      fails
```

Figure 4.12   The execution trace.

(c) The procedure 'member1' is better since it checks at each step whether the element is in the head of a list, while the procedure 'member2' first tries to find an element in the tail of a list.

16. If the order of the two clauses were changed, only powdered milk would get issued from stock.

17.
(a) X = 15
(b) X = 13
(c) max(X, Y, X) :- X >= Y.
    max(X, Y, Y) :- X < Y.

18. No. The first question forces the matching of X and Y which, therefore, become identical. The second question succeeds only if X and Y are identical. Take for example the following two facts:

```
f1( a( B)).
f2( a( b)).
```

The answer to the first question is:

```
X = a( b)
Y = a( b)
yes
```

and the answer to the second question is 'no'.

19.
```
most_general( Class) :-
   subclass( _, Class),
   not( subclass( Class, _)).
```

20.
(a) yes
(b) yes
(c) no
(d) no
(e) yes
(f) no

21. Yes, by the rule 'not_a_prime(X) :- not(prime(X))', because X is always already instantiated in a question.

22.
```
issue( milk, Litres, fresh, Litres) :-
   state( milk, fresh, L),
   L >= Litres,
   issued( milk, fresh, Litres).
issue( milk, Litres, powdered, Kilos) :-
   not(( state( milk, fresh, L), L >= Litres)),
   Kilos is Litres * 0.125,
   issued( milk, powdered, Kilos).
```

23.
```
very_good( Car, Price) :-
   car( Car, Fuel_cons, Accel, Price),
   Fuel_cons < 6.
very_good( Car, Price) :-
   car( Car, Fuel_cons, Accel, Price),
   Fuel_cons < 7,
   Accel < 10.

good( Car, Price) :-
   car( Car, Fuel_cons, Accel, Price),
   not( very_good( Car, Price)),
   Fuel_cons < 8,
   Accel < 13.
good( Car, Price) :-
   car( Car, Fuel_cons, Accel, Price),
   not( very_good( Car, Price)),
   Fuel_cons < 9,
   Accel < 12.
```

24.
(a) ?- not((person(X), likes(X, wine))).
(b) ?- not((person(X), not(likes(X, wine)))).
(c) ?- person(X), not((instrument(I), not(play(X, I)))).
(d) ?- not((person(X), not((instrument(I), play(X, I))))).
(e) ?- not((person(X), instrument(I), not(play(X, I)))).

25.
```
aunt( X, Y) :-
    parent( Z, Y),
    parent( G, Z),
    parent( G, X),
    Z \== X,
    female(X).
```

26.
```
:- op( 700, xfx, iss).

X iss Y :-
    ok( Y),
    X is Y.

ok( X) :- number( X).
ok( X) :-
    nonvar( X),            % fail if X is an uninstantiated variable
    not( atom( X)),        % fail if X is an atom
    X =.. [ H| Tail],      % if X is a structure
    oks( Tail).            % check the arguments

oks( []).
    oks( [ H| Tail]) :-
    ok( H),
    oks( Tail).
```

27.
```
convert( Kilometers, Miles) :-
    Miles iss Kilometers / 1.609. % see exercise 26
convert( Kilometers, Miles) :-
    Kilometers iss Miles * 1.609.
```

28.
```
sum( X, Y, Z) :-
    Z iss X + Y.           % see exercise 26
sum( X, Y, Z) :-
    X iss Z-Y.
sum( X, Y, Z) :-
    Y iss Z-X.
```

29. '\ = =' is the negation of '= =' and not of '='. If the operator '\ = =' was defined as in the exercise, the answer to the question
```
    ?- f( X) \== f( 1).
```
would be 'no', which is wrong.

Chapter 5

Programming Techniques

In this chapter we introduce some useful techniques which make Prolog a powerful programming tool, the most useful among them being recursive programming and the use of lists.

5.1 Recursive Programming

A Sample Recursive Program

Assume the results of a race are given by facts of the form 'before(Runner1, Runner2)', meaning that Runner1 reached the winning post immediately before Runner2. We want to define the relation 'better' for which 'better(X, Y)' is true if X finished the race before Y. Obviously, X is better than Y if X reached the winning post immediately before Y. This situation is illustrated in Figure 5.1 (a) and is covered by the following rule:

```
better( X, Y) :-
  before( X, Y).
```

X is also better than Y if X reached the winning post immediately before some Z that reached the post immediately before Y (see Figure 5.1 (b)):

```
better( X, Y) :-
  before( X, Z),
  before( Z, Y).
```

Of course, there may also be more than one runner between X and Y (see Figure 5.1 (c)). It would be very inconvenient if we had to write down all the rules describing the possible situations, for example:

```
better( X, Y) :-
    before( X, Z1),
    before( Z1, Z2),
    before( Z2, Y).
better( X, Y) :-
    before( X, Z1),
    before( Z1, Z2),
    before( Z2, Z3),
    before( Z3, Y).
...
```

Instead, let us try to find a more systematic solution to the problem. We should consider two cases. In the first case there is no other runner between X and Y. For this situation the predicate 'better/2' is defined by the rule:

```
better( X, Y) :-
    before( X, Y).
```

In the second case there are one or more runners between X and Y. Here we can define the predicate 'better/2' in terms of itself:

```
better( X, Y) :-
    before( X, Z),
    better( Z, Y).
```

What we get is a *recursive procedure*. The idea of defining a predicate recursively by using the same predicate in the body of the rule is illustrated in Figure 5.1 (d).

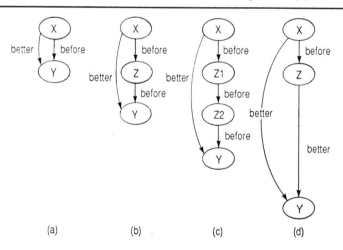

Figure 5.1   The relations 'better' and 'before'. In (d) we have a recursive definition of the relation 'better'.

The above recursive definition is somewhat similar to the one introduced in section 4.1:

```
nice :-
    nice.
```

which represents an endless loop. In fact, every recursive procedure is a potential endless loop, so it always needs a suitable *boundary condition* that will stop the execution. In our example the boundary condition is the case when there is no Z between X and Y, and so the rule:

```
better( X, Y) :-
   before( X, Y).
```

will stop the execution. The entire recursive procedure is thus the following:

```
better( X, Y) :-
   before( X, Y).
better( X, Y) :-
   before( X, Z),
   better( Z, Y).
```

Execution of a Recursive Program

Let us see how such a recursive program works. Suppose we have the following facts:

```
before( tom, tim).
before( tim, jack).
before( jack, jim).
before( jim, john).
```

and we are interested in knowing whether Tom is better than John:

```
?- better( tom, john).
```

The trace of the execution is shown in Figure 5.2.

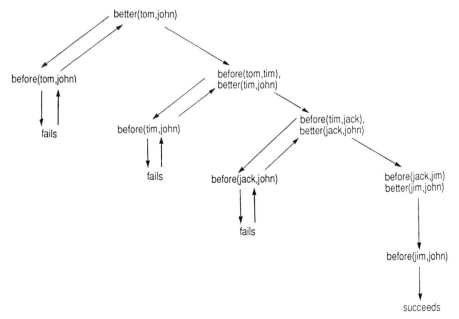

Figure 5.2 Execution trace of the recursive procedure 'better' answering the question 'better(tom, john)'.

In every iteration the boundary condition given in the first rule is tested first. If it fails, the recursive rule which takes into account some Z that is between X and Y is applied. If there is no such Z, the boundary condition is satisfied and the execution stops. If there is such Z, a *recursive call* of the procedure is executed. Note that if Z is between X and Y, then there are fewer runners between Z and Y than between X and Y. In every recursive call the number of intermediate runners is smaller. This guarantees that the execution will stop at the boundary condition. The reader should try to trace the execution of a question that will not succeed, for example:

```
?- better( tim, tom).
```

When will the execution stop?

Recursive arithmetic

Let us extend our program by adding information about the time difference between successive runners. We can do this by using facts such as:

```
before( tom, tim, 1.5).
```

saying that Tom reached the winning post 1.5 seconds before Tim. Can we extend the definition of the relation 'better' that will also return the difference in time? For example:

```
?- better( tom, tim, T).
T = 1.5
yes
```

The first rule can be simply extended:

```
better( X, Y, T) :-
    before( X, Y, T).
```

In the second rule we want to calculate the time difference by adding the time difference of Z to the leading time that was accumulated so far:

```
better( X, Y, T) :-
    before( X, Z, T1),
    better( Z, Y, T2),
    T is T1 + T2.
```

This gives us a recursive rule for calculating the time difference. Note that the third goal can not succeed unless both T1 and T2 are instantiated.

Most arithmetic operations are recursively defined. An illustrative example of a recursive definition is that of the factorial of natural numbers. The factorial of n is defined by:

```
n! = n*(n-1)*(n-2)* ... *2*1
```

or recursively by:

```
0! = 1
n! = n*(n-1)!
```

82

which can be directly written in Prolog:

```
factorial( 0, 1).
factorial( N, F) :-
    N > 0,
    N1 is N-1,
    factorial( N1, F1),
    F is N * F1.
```

The boundary condition is given in the first rule and is satisfied for n = 0.

Exercises

1. Define the following procedures using facts of the form 'child(X, Y)'.
(a)   ancestor(Ancestor, Offspring).
(b)   offspring(Offspring, Predecessor).
(c)   blood_relation(X, Y).

2. Write recursive Prolog procedures that define the following arithmetic operations on natural numbers:
(a)   'exp(N, X, Y)' where Y is X raised to the power of N, i.e. X*X*..*X N-times.
(b)   'mod(X, Y, Z)' where Z is the remainder of the integer division of X by Y.
(c)   'fib(N, X)' where X is the N-th element of the Fibonacci sequence, i.e. 0, 1, 1, 2, 3, 5, 8, 13, ... (each element is the sum of the preceding two).
(d)   (*) 'between(X, Min, Max)', which will return, by backtracking, all X which are between the numbers Min and Max.
(e)   (**) 'prime(X)', which will return, by backtracking, all prime numbers.

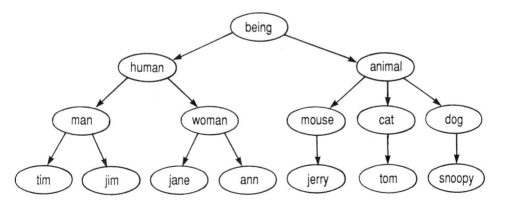

Figure 5.3 (a)   The tree representation of the relation 'is'.

3.
(a)   Define the trees in Figures 5.3 with a set of facts of the form
(a1) 'is(X, Y)' for the tree 5.3 (a).
(a2) 'one_part_is(X, Y)' for the tree 5.3 (b).

(b)   Write the recursive Prolog procedures of the form
(b1) 'is_a(X, Y)' for the tree 5.3 (a).
(b2) 'a_part_of(X, Y)' for the tree 5.3 (b).

(c)   (**) Could we use in (b) the same name for facts and for recursive procedures as in
      (a)?

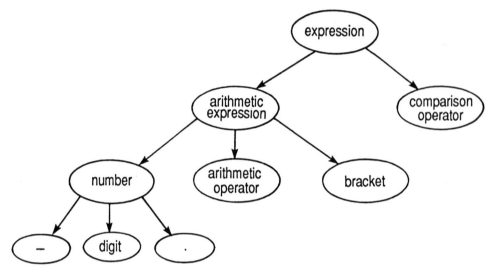

Figure 5.3 (b)   The tree representation of the relation 'one_part_is'.

4. Are the following procedures correct:
(a)
```
better( X, Y) :-
    before( X, Y).
better( X, Y) :-
    better( Z, Y),
    before( X, Z).
```
(b) (*)
```
better( X, Y) :-
    before( X, Y).
better( X, Y) :-
    better( Z, Y),
    better( X, Z).
```
(c) (*)
```
better( X, Y) :-
    before( X, Y).
better( X, Y) :-
    better( X, Z),
    better( Z, Y).
```

84

5.

(a) (*) Define the procedure 'equal/2' so that the goal 'equal(X, Y)' succeeds if two runners X and Y finished the race at the same time.

(b) (*) Define the procedure 'better1/2' so that 'better1(X, Y, T)' will also be correctly defined for T = < 0, where 'better1(X, Y, T)' is the same as 'better1(Y, X, −T)'.

6. The theory of critical path analysis is used to evaluate projects, which are determined by sets of tasks that have to be performed. Each task is determined by a fact:

```
task( Name, Duration, List_of_tasks).
```

The third argument is a list of tasks that have to be finished before the current task named 'Name' is to be undertaken. Beside facts of the above form let us also have a fact:

```
tasks( List_of_all_tasks).
```

(a) Define the procedure 'start_task(Task)' that succeeds if the 'Task' can start immediately at the beginning of the project.

(b) (**) Define a procedure 'duration(T)' which will return the minimal possible duration time of a whole project. (Hint: define the procedures 'earliest_start(Task, Start)' and 'earliest_finish(Task, Finish)' to compute the earliest possible starting and finishing times of the 'Task'.)

5.2. Using Lists

Lists are a *recursive data structure*. They are defined recursively: a list consists of a head and a tail which is also a list. A natural consequence of such a definition is that most operations on lists are defined recursively. The most frequent operations on lists are searching for an element of a list and concatenating two lists.

Membership

The membership relation is defined by the procedure 'member/2'. The goal 'member(X, L)' succeeds if X is an element of list L. For example, the goals 'member(3, [1,2,3])' and 'member([2], [[1], [2], [3]])' should succeed, while the goal 'member(2, [1, [2,3]])' should not. The procedure that implements the 'member' relation is the following:

```
member( X, [ X| _ ]).
member( X, [ _| Tail]) :-
    member( X, Tail).
```

This definition of the 'member' relation states that X is a member of a list if X is the head of a list or if it is a member of the tail. The boundary condition defined in the first clause is satisfied when an element is found in the head of a list. A recursive call in the second clause searches for an element in the tail of a list that is shorter than the original list. Therefore, if an element is in a list, the boundary condition definitely will 'fire'. If an element is not in a list, the inspected part of the list will, after a certain number of recursive calls, become empty and the procedure will not succeed, since no head of a clause will match the goal.

The procedure can also be used in two other ways: to obtain an arbitrary element of a list; or to construct a list of arbitrary length containing a given element in some position. An element can be any Prolog structure and even an uninstantiated variable. Note that a list of arbitrary length is obtained if we have a variable in place of the tail (see Note 3 of section 3.3 on how to obtain and treat unbounded lists).

Concatenation

The concatenation of two lists is defined by the procedure 'conc(L1, L2, L3)' where L3 is a list obtained by concatenating the lists L1 and L2. For example:

```
conc( [1,2], [3,4], [1,2,3,4])
```
is true. The procedure is the following:

```
conc( [], L, L).
conc( [ X| L1], L2, [ X| L3]) :-
   conc( L1, L2, L3).
```

The definition states that the concatenation of an empty list with any list results in the list itself. The concatenation of a list having head X and tail L1 with any list L2 results in the list whose head is X and whose tail is obtained by concatenating L1 and L2. The situation covered by the second clause is illustrated in Figure 5.4.

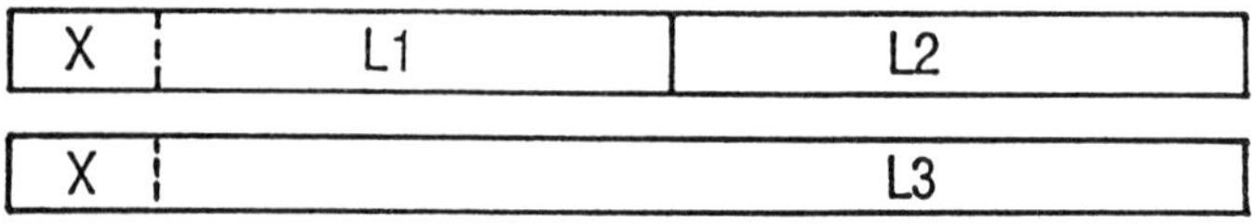

Figure 5.4   Concatenation of two lists.

In this procedure the boundary condition is satisfied when the first list is empty. The recursive call shortens the first list by one element, which guarantees the termination of the execution.

Different Uses of the Procedure 'conc'

The procedure 'conc(L1, L2, L3)' can be used to concatenate two lists L1 and L2 into L3 or to obtain an arbitrary partitioning of a list L3 into two sublists L1 and L2. In this way, the procedure may also be used to implement the 'member' relation:

```
member( X, List) :-
   conc( _, [ X| _], List).
```

The procedure says that X is a member of a List if it is in the head of some right part of List.

We can also use the procedure for deleting an element from a list:

```
delete( X, List, Result) :-
    conc( L1, [ X| L2], List),
    conc( L1, L2, Result).
```

This procedure says that in order to delete an element X from List, X should first be found as the head of some right part of List, thus partitioning the list in two sublists L1 and L2. By concatenating L1 and L2, Result is obtained.

Let us show how to use the procedure 'conc' to insert an element into an arbitrary position of a list:

```
insert( X, List, Result) :-
    delete( X, Result, List).
```

The procedure may be also used to return (and to search for) an arbitrary sublist of a given list:

```
sublist( List, Sublist) :-
    conc( _, L1, List),
    conc( Sublist, _, L1).
```

Sublist is obtained as a left part of some right part of List.

Searching Graphs

A *graph* is defined by a set of *nodes* and *edges* between them. A *directed graph* is a graph in which all the edges have a direction from one node to the other and may be called *arcs*. Look at the directed graph shown in Figure 5.5.

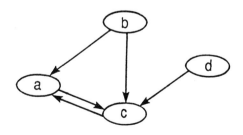

Figure 5.5 A directed graph.

The graph is described by the following facts:

```
arc( a, c).
arc( a, b).
arc( c, a).
arc( c, b).
arc( c, d).
```

Let us define a procedure 'path(X, Y)' which is true if there is a path (consisting of a sequence of arcs) between the nodes X and Y:

```
path( X, Y) :-
   arc( X, Y).
path( X, Y) :-
   arc( X, Z),
   path( Z, Y).
```

If we now ask the question:

```
?- path( a, d).
```

Prolog will endlessly search for a path from a to d because of the infinite loop a -> c -> a. To overcome this problem we introduce an additional argument, 'Trail', which enables us to check whether we have already examined a certain node when searching for a path:

```
path( X, Y) :-              % At the beginning
   path( X, Y, []).         % the Trail is empty.
path( X, Y, _) :-
   arc( X, Y).
path( X, Y, Trail) :-
   arc( X, Z),
   not( member( Z, Trail)),    % Z is not yet examined
   path( Z, Y, [ X| Trail]).   % X is already examined.
```

Notes

1. We have defined a procedure for deleting an element from a list with the use of the procedure 'conc'. Note that a more efficient procedure for deleting an element from a list finds and deletes the element as the head of some sublist:

```
delete( X, [ X| Tail], Tail).
delete( X, [ Y| Tail], [ Y| Tail1]) :-
   delete( X, Tail, Tail1).
```

2. We had a procedure for inserting an element in an arbitrary position of a list. The simplest procedure for adding an element to a list is by putting it in front of the other elements:

```
add( X, List, [ X| List]).
```

3. We often want to perform a certain transformation on all elements of a list. For example, let us define the procedure 'squares(Numbers, Squares)' that gives us squares of numbers in a given list:

88

```
squares( [], []).
squares( [ N| Tail], [S | Stail]) :-
    S is N * N,
    squares( Tail, Stail).
```

n general, we have a predicate 'Transform/2' which performs the desired transformation on
he elements of a list. The transformation of the entire list is called also the *mapping of a list*:

```
map( [], _, []).
map( [ H| Tail], Transform, [ MH| MTail]) :-
    Goal =.. [ Transform, H, MH],
    call( Goal),
    map( Tail, Transform, MTail).
```

Syntactically, a predicate is a functor, therefore we may use the operator ' =..' to construct
Goal to transform the head of a list H into the head of a transformed list MH. We use a built-
in procedure *'call/1'* to force the execution of constructed Goal. Suppose we have the
following procedure:

```
f( X, X * X).
```

hen we obtain the following answer to the question:

```
?- map( [1, 2, a, b, 3], f, X).
X = [ 1*1, 2*2, a*a, b*b, 3*3]
yes
```

Exercises

7. Define the following procedures:
a) 'longer_than(List1, List2)' – List1 is longer than List2
b) 'length(List, Length)'-Length is the number of elements in List
c) 'member(X, List, N)' – List contains N occurences of X.

8. Define the following procedures:
a) (*) 'is_a_list(Structure)' – Structure is a list
b) 'is_a_set(List)' – List is a set (i.e. each element appears in List only once)
c) (*) 'make_set(List, Set)' – Set is a list containing every element in List only once.

9. Define the following procedures:
a) 'union(Set1, Set2, Union)' – Union of sets Set1 and Set2
b) 'intersection(Set1, Set2, Intersection)' – Intersection of sets Set1 and Set2
c) (**) 'power_set(Set, Power)' – Power is the power set of Set, i.e. the set of all subsets
of Set.

10. (*) Define the procedure 'reverse(List, Reversed)' that will return a reversed list. Use the
procedure 'conc', defined in this section.

11. (*) For a directed graph define the procedure 'exists_path(X, Y, Path)' that will return
also a path, i.e. a list of nodes between X and Y, including X and Y. Use the facts in the form
arc(X, Y)'.

12. (**) In exercise 6 we introduced the project problem. Define the procedure 'critical__path(Path)' that will return a critical path. It is defined as a list of tasks that must be performed immediately one after another in order to finish the project in a minimal possible time. If we delay the start of any task from the critical path, the entire project will be delayed.

5.3 Simulating Global Variables

It is common practice in procedural programming to use global variables, i.e. variables that are accessible from the entire program. In Prolog there are no global variables as all variables are local, limited to the clause in which they appear.

Two built-in procedures 'assert/1' and 'retract/1' are provided to enable modifying programs and data by adding and deleting program clauses. This can be also used for simulating *global variables*.

The goal 'assert(Clause)' adds Clause to the current program; it always succeeds. The goal 'retract(Clause)' deletes the first clause that matches Clause. If there is no such clause, 'retract' fails. Usually, two types of the procedure 'assert' are available: 'asserta' for adding a clause at the beginning of a program and 'assertz' for adding a clause at the end of a program.

We already know that Prolog does not distinguish between program and data. As Prolog has no global variables, the procedure 'assert' has to be used in order to save a value of a variable (computed during the execution of a program) by adding a fact to the program with the goal 'assert(value(Variable__name, Value))', for example:

```
assert( value( x, 5))
```

Now we can simply obtain the value of the variable by the query:

```
?- value( x, Value).
Value = 5
yes
```

All procedural languages have some means for storing and changing values of variables. Prolog can not change the value of a variable except when backtracking. In order to change the value of a variable stored by 'assert' we can use the following procedure:

```
change( Variable, New_value) :-
  retract( value( Variable, _)),
  assert( value( Variable, New_value)).
```

We may want to store already computed values of variables obtained as answers to some query. If the procedure which computes the answer is time consuming, it is especially useful to use 'asserta' for storing the results. In this way, when a result is already computed it is immediately retrieved as a fact and computation only takes place when there is no result available.

Let us consider, for example, the procedure 'check__divide(X)' which succeeds if X is not a prime number (see exercise 13). Since the procedure is time consuming it is useful to save the so far obtained results. We therefore define another procedure as follows:

```
not_prime( X) :-
    check_divide( X),
    asserta( not_prime( X)).
```

If X is not a prime then the goal 'check__divide(X)' will succeed and a fact will be added to the program in front of the procedure 'not__prime'. If Prolog later tries to satisfy the goal 'not__prime(X)' for the same value of X, the procedure 'check__divide' will not have to be invoked, because the goal will immediately succeed.

We might also store results in the form 'result(Value)'. We may wish to collect them later into a list by the procedure 'collect(List)':

```
collect( [ X| Tail]) :-
    retract( result( X)),
    collect( Tail).
collect( []).                    % If 'retract' fails there are no
                                 % more results.
```

Exercises

3. (*) Define the procedure 'check__divide(X)'.

4. Define the procedure 'increase__price(Article, Percentage)' which will
a) increase the price of a certain Article by a given Percentage in a knowledge base of facts of the form 'price(Article, Price)'.
b) increase the price of all articles by a given Percentage in a knowledge base of facts of the form 'price(Article, Price)'.

5. What does the following procedure do?

```
l( L, N) :-
    l( L),
    retract( n( N)).
l( []) :-
    assert( n( 0)).
l( [ _| L]) :-
    l( L),
    retract( n( N)),
    N1 is N + 1,
    assert( n( N1)).
```

6. (*) Define a procedure 'findall(Element, Goals, List)' that will return List of Elements satisfying Goals.

7. Let us define a state in the block world of a robot with a set of facts of the form
'on(X, Y)' — a block X is on Y, where Y is a block or the floor
'handempty' — the robot's hand is empty
'holding(X)' — the robot is holding a block X

Define the following procedures which change the state of the block world:
(a) 'pickup(X)' − the robot picks up block X
(b) 'put(X, Y)' − put block X on Y
(c) (*) 'clear(X)' − remove all blocks from block X

Before an action is performed, some preconditions must hold: for example, before the 'pickup' operation 'handempty' must be true. If an action can not be executed, the procedure should fail without changing the state. Figure 5.6 shows how the state of the world changes after the question:

```
?- pickup( a), put( a, floor), pickup( b).
```

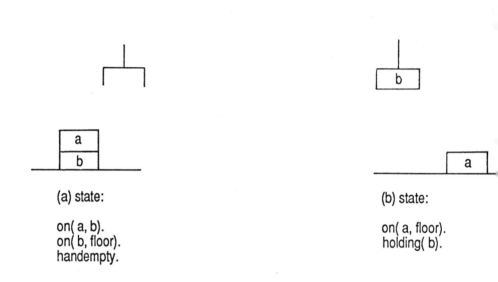

(a) state:

on(a, b).
on(b, floor).
handempty.

(b) state:

on(a, floor).
holding(b).

Figure 5.6 A state (a) in the robot's block world changes to (b) after the conjunction of goals 'pickup(a), put(a, floor), pickup(b)' is executed.

5.4 Controlling Backtracking With 'Cut'

We use the procedure 'member', introduced in section 5.2, for searching for an element of a list. If there are several elements in a list that match a given element, Prolog returns, through backtracking, all of them. For example:

```
?- member( f(X), [ f(1), g(2), f(3), g(4)]).
X = 1;
X = 3;
no
```

If we know in advance that each element appears, at most, once in the list (for example, when the list represents a set), we know that backtracking can be avoided since it is a useless, time and memory consuming operation. On the other hand, we may sometimes want a procedure to find only one solution, although there may be several solutions of the problem. In order to obtain a single solution, we can use the *cut*, denoted by the exclamation mark '!'. As a goal, the cut succeeds immediately and can not be resatisfied. When backtracking returns to the cut the *parent goal* is forced to fail, i.e. the goal that matched the head of the clause containing the cut. Therefore the cut affects the way backtracking works after the cut succeeds. The cut is used to tell the interpreter which alternative choices it need not consider when it backtracks through the chain of satisfied goals. Using the cut, we define the procedure 'member1' as follows:

```
member1( X, [ X| _]) :- !.
member1( X, [ _| Tail]) :-
  member1( X, Tail).
```

To illustrate the difference between 'member' and 'member1', let us ask the same question as above. Prolog will return only the first solution:

```
?- member1( f(X), [ f(1), g(2), f(3), g(4)]).
X = 1;
no
```

After the solution was found by the first clause, the cut succeeds. By typing in a semi-colon, backtracking is invoked and the cut forces a failure of the parent goal in question, therefore Prolog does not return any other solution.

A Detailed Explanation of the Effects of 'Cut'

The cut represents a goal that succeeds immediately and commits Prolog to all the choices made since the parent goal was matched (with the head of the clause in which cut occurs) up to the time the cut was encountered.

Let us illustrate the effects of the cut on the following example. Suppose that we have the following three clauses:

```
B :- E, F, !, G, H.
B :- K.
X :- A, B, C, D.
```

The effects of the cut are the following:

a) Cut discards all alternative solutions of the conjunction of goals to the left of the cut. This means that the goals followed by the cut may produce at most one solution (i.e. backtracking is possible within the goals 'E' and 'F', but as soon as both 'E' and 'F' succeed and the cut is encountered, these two goals can't be resatisfied; therefore, all remaining solutions are discarded).

b) Cut discards all clauses below it. If the goal 'B' succeeds through the first clause (i.e. if the goals 'E', 'F', 'G' and 'H' succeed) we can not obtain solutions using clauses with the same head 'B' below the clause containing the cut (i.e. solutions obtained by the possible successes of 'K' are discarded).

(c) The cut does not affect the goals to its right in the clause. They may produce more than one solution while backtracking (i.e. if all the goals in the first clause are satisfied, goals 'G' and 'H' may get resatisfied when backtracking).

(d) Once the parent goal fails, backtracking proceeds from the last goal prior to the parent goal. If the parent goal of the clause containing the cut 'B' is in the clause:

```
X :- A, B, C, D.
```

the cut will only affect the execution of the goal 'B', while the execution of the others is unchanged (e.g. backtracking within the goal 'A' remains active).

Effects of 'Cut' on the Declarative Meaning

Obviously, the cut from the procedure 'member1' can be removed without affecting the procedural correctness of the procedure. Such cut is called a *green cut*.

Sometimes it is useful to change also the declarative semantics of a procedure in order to eliminate redundant computations. Let us define the procedure 'max' for finding maximal number in a list of numbers:

```
max( 0, []).
max( X, [X]).
max( X, [ X| Tail]) :-
  max( M, Tail),
  M =< X.
max( M, [ X| Tail]) :-
  max( M, Tail),
  M > X.
```

Prolog would often have to compute the maximal element of a Tail twice if the maximal element is not in the head of a list. We can change the order of the second and the third clause to make the procedure more efficient, since, in general, there is a greater probability that the maximal element of a list is in the tail. Still, this doesn't solve the problem of redundant computations. The problem is solved by using the cut:

```
max( 0, []).
max( X, [X]).
max( M, [ X| Tail]) :-
  max( M, Tail),
  M >= X, !.
max( X, [ X| _]).
```

If the cut were removed, the procedure would through backtracking return incorrect solutions. Declaratively, the last clause is incorrect and can be correctly used only in an appropriate position within the procedure. The order of the third and the fourth clause in the procedure may now not be changed. A cut that can not be removed without affecting the procedural correctness is called a *red cut*.

Defining Negation with 'Cut' and 'fail'

With the use of the cut and the built-in procedure 'fail' that immediately fails, it is possible to define the 'negation as failure' introduced in section 4.4:

```
not( Goal) :-
    call( Goal), !,
    fail.
not( _).
```

If Goal succeeds, the procedure will fail and vice versa (provided that Goal does not lead to an infinite loop).

Exercises

18. In exercise 16 of section 4.3 we defined a procedure for issuing milk from a hotel storage. The correction of the declarative reading using 'not' (exercise 22, section 4.4) contained redundant computations. Correct the procedure using the cut to exclude both redundant and incorrect computation through backtracking.

19. (**) Define the procedure 'same_var(X, Y)' that will succeed if X and Y represent the same uninstantiated variable.

5.5 Input and Output

So far we have considered the user's communication with a Prolog program in the form of questions and the program's answers in a dialogue via a computer terminal. In this case the keyboard of a terminal is the so called *current input stream* from which all *input* is *read*, and the screen of a terminal is the *current output stream* to which all *output* is *written*. The terminal is a special default input and output stream usually named *'user'.*

Input and Output of Terms

At the beginning of a communication, the current input and output streams are set to the user's terminal. The goals 'read(Term)' and 'write(Term)' are used to read and write terms from/to the input and output stream. In the input stream, terms must be terminated by a period.

We often use 'read' and 'write' to program a dialogue with a user. 'Write' is used for displaying questions and results, and 'read' is used for reading data that a user types in. The following procedure executes user's commands until the user enters the command 'stop':

```
do :-
    write('command: '),
    read( Command),
    perform( Command).

perform( stop) :- !.
perform( Command) :-
    execute( Command),        % 'execute' is assumed to be given
    do.                       % ask for the next command
```

Sometimes we want to write several terms, one after another. For example, the procedure 'write_colour(X)' will write a sentence about the colour of X:

```
write_colour( X) :-
    colour( X, Colour),
    write( 'The colour of '),
    write( X),
    write( 'is '),
    write( Colour).
    write( '.'),
    nl.                          % continue in a new line
```

The goal 'nl' is a built-in procedure that causes a new line to be started on the current output stream.

All input and output operations are deterministic in that (while backtracking) they can not be resatisfied. Therefore the answer to a question:

```
?- write( 'hello'), fail.
```

will be:

```
hello
no
```

and not:

```
hellohellohello ...
```

By the question:

```
?- read( X), write( X), fail.
```

we may read only one term from the current input stream. The conjunction of goals will then fail since the goal 'read(X)' can not be resatisfied.

Directing Input and Output to Files

It is often useful to direct input and output to files (ASCII coded character files). Each file has a *filename* that must be a Prolog atom. If we want to read from a file named Filename, we have to switch the current input stream (which is initially the user's terminal) to the new one by the goal:

```
see( Filename)
```

For example:

```
see( 'data.txt')
```

where single quotes are used to build an atom. If a file is already opened for reading, then the goal 'see(Filename)' simply switches the current input stream to that file. The goal:

```
seen
```

96

will close the current input stream and switch it back to 'user'. The following procedure will display terms from file Filename as long as required by the user:

```
display( Filename) :-
   see( Filename),
   read( Term),
   write( Term), nl,
   see( user),
   write( 'More terms: (y/n)'),
   read( Yes_No),
   perform( Yes_No, Filename).


perform( n, _) .
perform( _, Filename) :-
   display( Filename).
```

The goal 'see(Filename)' succeeds only once and cannot be resatisfied when backtracking. The first time this goal is satisfied for some Filename, the file is opened. Reading of terms is started at the beginning of the file and subsequently continued until the file is closed by the goal 'seen'. If, during the execution of a program, the goal 'see(Filename)' succeeds again, reading is again started from the beginning of the file. If Filename is not instantiated or is instantiated to a filename that does not exist the goal fails. The name of the current input stream may be obtained by the goal 'seeing(Filename)'.

If we want to write on a file, we have to assign the current output stream to it. This is achieved with the goal 'tell(Filename)'. If a file is already opened for writing, the goal 'tell(Filename)' will simply switch the current output stream to that file. The goal 'told' will close the file and change the current output stream back to the 'user'. The following procedure will copy the terms, typed in by the user, each in a new line to the file Filename until 'stop' is entered:

```
copy( Filename) :-
   tell( user),
   write( 'Term: '),
   read( Term),
   tell( Filename),
   perform( Term, Filename).


perform( stop, _) :- told.
perform( Term, Filename) :-
   write( Term), nl,
   copy( Filename).
```

If the argument of the procedure 'tell' is not instantiated, the goal 'tell(Filename)' fails. If the argument is instantiated to a filename that does not exist, a file of that name is created and all output is subsequently directed to it. If Filename is instantiated to the name of an existing file, the content of this file will be destroyed.

Input and Output of Characters

It is possible to read and write also single characters. The goal:

```
get0( X)
```

reads a single character from the current input stream and instantiates X to an integer that represents the ASCII code of that character. In contrast with 'get0/1', whose argument may be any ASCII character, the procedure 'get/1' operates only on printing characters (those that have ASCII codes greater than 32). The goal:

```
put( X)
```

writes a single character with the ASCII code X on the current output stream. X must be instantiated to an integer. The procedures 'get', 'get0' and 'put' can only succeed once and can not be resatisfied.

The following procedure will copy a sentence (terminated with a period) from a file Input to a file Output:

```
copy_sentence( Input, Output) :-
  see( Input),
  tell( Output),
  copy,
  seen,
  told.

copy :-
  get0( Ch),
  put( Ch),
  treat( [Ch]).

treat( ".").           % In case of a period the execution should
treat( _) :-           % stop with success. Note that we used the
  copy.                % string notation as introduced in
                       % section 3.3.
```

Instead of the procedures 'seen' and 'told', the goal 'close(Filename)' can be used to close the file for input and output. When reading from an input file, the end of the file may possibly be reached. In this case, 'read(X)' will instantiate X to the atom 'end_of_file' and the next call of 'read(X)' will fail. If the end of file is reached, 'get0(X)' will fail immediately. Note that different Prolog implementations treat this case in different ways.

Consulting

Files are used to store programs, i.e. programs and data, since there is no distinction between the two in Prolog. A program may be stored on several files, each *module* on a separate file. A module is a part of a program containing procedures for solving a particular problem or problems of a certain type.

If a module of the program is stored in a file F, we can read all the clauses in the file and add them to our program with the goal:

```
consult( F)
```

Most Prolog implementations have a special notation for consulting files, which allows a list of files to be consulted, one after another. In programs that consist of several modules, we typically use this feature in a command defined in the first clause of the main module in order to consult files containing different modules, for example:

```
?- ['data.txt', module1, module2].
```

The goal 'reconsult(F)' has the same effect as 'consult(F)' except that before adding the procedures from file F to the current program, all the procedures that exist both in the program and in file F are erased from the program.

A built-in procedure 'listing(P)' displays the clauses with the procedure name P regardless of how many arguments the procedure has. The procedure 'listing' may be used also without an argument. In this case it lists all the clauses in the current program to the current output stream.

The following example illustrates the above notions. Suppose that the file 'plays' contains the following program:

```
plays( X, Y) :-
    plays( X, Y, _).
plays( X, organ) :-
    plays( X, piano).
plays( X, piano) :-
    plays( X, accordion).
```

Suppose that the contents of a file named 'beatles' is the following:

```
plays( john, guitar, rhythm).
plays( george, guitar, solo).
plays( paul, guitar, bass).
plays( ringo, drums).
```

The following dialogue illustrates the use of the procedures 'consult', 'reconsult' and 'listing'.

```
?- listing.
yes
?- consult( beatles).
yes
?- listing.
plays( john, guitar, rhythm).
plays( george, guitar, solo).
plays( paul, guitar, bass).
plays( ringo, drums).
yes
?- reconsult( plays).
yes
```

```
?- listing.
plays( john, guitar, rhythm).
plays( george, guitar, solo).
plays( paul, guitar, bass).

plays( X, Y) :-
    plays( X, Y, ).
plays( X, organ) :-
    plays( X, piano).
plays( X, piano) :-
    plays( X, accordion).
yes
```

Note that the clause 'plays(ringo, drums)' was erased from the program because of the use of 'reconsult'.

Exercises

20. Define the procedure 'write__list(List)' that will successively write the terms of List, in the order, in which they appear in it. If a term in a list is 'nl', then writing will continue on a new line. If a term is 'tab(N)', N spaces will be output. Other terms must be written literally.

21. Define the procedure 'copy(Input, Output)' that copies file Input to file Output.

22. Change the procedure 'parent' from section 1.2 so that it will produce the following dialogue:
```
?- parent.
Whose parent are you searching for? jane.
The parent of jane is ann.
yes
```

23. (*) Define the procedure 'consult1(File, Predicate-name)' that will add all clauses of procedure Predicate-name with N arguments from file File to the current program.

5.6 Summary

—A recursive procedure is obtained if a predicate is defined in terms of itself. Such a procedure contains also a recursive call and a boundary condition. The execution of a recursive procedure leads through a sequence of recursive calls until the boundary condition is fulfilled.

—Most list operations are defined recursively. Usually, each successive recursive call operates on a shorter list and the boundary condition is fulfilled when the list is empty.

—The built-in procedures 'assert' and 'retract' are used for adding and deleting clauses to/from the current program. This facility can be used to simulate global variables, to update a database and to store results in order to avoid unnecessary recomputation of the same results.

—Cut is used to improve the efficiency of programs and to discard alternative solutions. Green cuts are preferred to red cuts, since they can be removed without altering the procedural correctness of programs.

—The built-in procedures 'read' and 'write' are used to read and write Prolog terms. Terms are read from the current input stream and written to the current output stream. By default, the current input/output stream is the user's terminal. The procedures 'get0' and 'put' are used to read and write single characters.

—The built-in procedures 'see' and 'tell' are used for opening files for reading and writing and for switching the current input/output stream to files and back to the user's terminal. The procedures 'seen' and 'told' are used for closing files.

—The built-in procedure 'consult(F)' is used to add a program from file F to the current program. 'reconsult(F)' has the same effect as 'consult(F)' except that before adding the procedures from file F to the current program, all the procedures that exist both in the program and in file F are erased from the program.

5.7 Solutions to Exercises

1.
(a)
```
ancestor( X, Y) :-
    child( Y, X).
ancestor( X, Y) :-
    child( Y, Y1),
    ancestor( X, Y1).
```
(b)
```
offspring( X, Y) :-
    ancestor( Y, X).            % see (a)
```
(c)
```
blood_relation( X, Y) :-
    ancestor( X, Y);            % see (a)
    ancestor( Y, X);
    same_ancestor( X, Y).

same_ancestor( X, Y) :-
    ancestor( Z, X),
    ancestor( Z, Y),
    X \== Y.
```

2.
(a)
```
exp( _, 0, 1).
exp( 0, _, 0).
exp( X, N, Y) :-
    N1 is N-1,
    exp( X, N1, Y1),
    Y is Y1 * X.
```

```
(b)  mod( X, Y, X) :-
        X < Y.
     mod( X, Y, Z) :-
        W is X-Y,
        mod( W, Y, Z).
(c)  fib( 0, 1).
     fib( 1, 1).
     fib( N, F) :-
        N1 is N-1,
        fib( N1, F1),
        N2 is N-2,
        fib( N2, F2),
        F is F1 + F2.
(d)  between( X, Min, Max) :-
        X is Min + 1,
        X < Max.
     between( X, Min, Max) :-
        Min1 is Min + 1,
        Min1 < Max,
        between( X, Min1, Max).
(e)  prime( X) :-
        next( 1, Y),
        check( Y),
        X = Y.
     next( X, X1) :-
        X1 is X + 1.
     next( X, X1) :-
        next( X, X2),
        X1 is X2 + 1.
     check( P) :-
        not(( between( X, 1, P)),   % see (d)
             0 is P mod X)).



3.
(a1) is( tim, man).
     is( jim, man).
     is( jane, woman).
     is( ann, woman).
     is( man, human).
     is( woman, human).
     is( jerry, mouse).
     is( tom, cat).
     is( snoopy, dog).
     is( mouse, animal).
     is( cat, animal).
     is( dog, animal).
     is( human, being).
     is( animal, being).
```

```
(a2) one_part_is( '-', number).
     one_part_is( digit, number).
     one_part_is( '.', number).
     one_part_is( number, arith_expr).
     one_part_is( arith_op, arith_expr).
     one_part_is( bracket, arith_exp).
     one_part_is( arith_exp, expr).
     one_part_is( comp_op, expr).
(b1) is_a( X, Y) :-
        is( X, Y).
     is_a( X, Y) :-
        is( X, Z),
        is_a( Z, Y).
(b2) a_part_of( X, Y) :-
        one_part_is( X, Y).
     a_part_of( X, Y) :-
        one_part_is( X, Z),
        a_part_of( Z, Y).
```

(c) No. If the same name is used for a recursive procedure as for facts, the program may possibly find some solutions by the first clause of the procedure but will then enter into an infinite loop.

4.
(a) yes
(b) no. Once the first goal in the second clause is satisfied, it can never be satisfied again (see also exercise 3 (c)).
(c) no. See (b).

5.
(a)
```
equal( X, Y) :-
    runner( X),
    runner( Y),
    not( better( X, Y)),    % see exercise 4(a)
    not( better( Y, X)).

runner( X) :-               % We assume that all runners
    before( X, _);          % will not reach the winning
    before( _, X).          % post at the same time.
```

(b)
```
better1( X, Y, T) :-
    better( X, Y, T).
better1( X, Y, T) :-
    better( Y, X, T1),
    T is -T1.
better1( X, Y, 0) :-
    equal( X, Y).           % see (a)
```

6.
(a)
```
start_task( Task) :-
    task( Task, _, []).
```

103

```
(b)   duration( T) :-
         tasks( List),
         earliest_fins( List, Fins),
            max( Fins, T).

         earliest_fins( [], []).
         earliest_fins( [ Task| List], [ Fin| Fins] ) :-
            earliest_finish( Task, Fin),
            earliest_fins( List, Fins).

         earliest_finish( Task, Fin) :-
            task( Task, D, _),
            earliest_start( Task, Start),
            Fin is Start + D.

         earliest_start( Task, Start) :-
            task( Task, D, List),
            earliest_fins( List, Fins),
            max( Fins, Start).

         max( [], 0).
         max( [X], X).
         max( [ X| Tail], Max) :-
            max( Tail, Max),
            Max >= X.
         max(.[ X| _], X).


7.
(a)   longer_than( [ _| _], []).
      longer_than( [ _| Tail], [ _| Tail1]) :-
         longer_than( Tail, Tail1).
(b)   length( [], 0).
      length( [ _| Tail], N) :-
         length( Tail, N1),
         N is N1 + 1.
(c)   member( X, [], 0).
      member( X, [ X| Tail], N) :-
         member( X, Tail, N1),
         N is N1 + 1.
      member( X, [ _| Tail], N) :-
         member( X, Tail, N).


8.
(a)   is_a_list( []).
      is_a_list( [ _| Tail]) :-
         is_a_list( Tail).
(b)   is_a_set( []).
      is_a_set( [ X| Tail]) :-
         not( member( X, Tail)),
         is_a_set( Tail).
```

```
(c)   make_set( [], []).
      make_set( [ X| Tail], Set) :-
         member( X, Tail),
         make_set( Tail, Set).
      make_set( [ X| Tail], [ X| Set]) :-
         make_set( Tail, Set).
```

9.
```
(a)   union( [], Set, Set).
      union( [ X| Tail], Set, Union) :-
         member( X, Set),
         union( Tail, Set, Union).
      union( [ X| Tail], Set, [ X| Union]) :-
         union( Tail, Set, Union).
(b)   intersection( [], _, []).
      intersection( [ X| Tail], Set, [ X| Int]) :-
         member( X, Set),
         intersection( Tail, Set, Int).
      intersection( [ _| Tail], Set, Int) :-
         intersection( Tail, Set, Int).
(c)   power_set( [], [[]]).
      power_set( [ X| Set], Power) :-
         power_set( Set, Power1),
         add( X, Power1, Power).
      /* Make an additional copy of every subset by adding a
         new element. */
      add( _, [], []).
      add( X, [ S| Power1], [ S, [ X| S]| Power]) :-
         add( X, Power1, Power).
```

10.
```
      reverse( [], []).
      reverse( [ X| Tail], Reversed) :-
         reverse( Tail, Rev1),
         conc( Rev1, [X], Reversed).        % see section 5.2
```

11.
```
      exists_path( X, Y, Path) :-
         exists_path( X, Y, Path, []).      % The fourth argument is
      exists_path( X, Y, Path, Trail) :- % the current trail.
         arc( X, Y),
         reverse( [Y, X| Trail], Path).     % see exercise 10
      exists_path( X, Y, Path, Trail) :-
         arc( X, Z),
         not( member( Z, Trail)),
         exists_path( Z, Y, Path, [ X| Trail]).
```

12. We search for a critical path in reverse order, starting at the end of a project and searching for a task whose earliest possible finish time equals the finish time of the whole project. Then progressing backwards by searching for a task whose earliest possible finish time equals the earliest possible start of the current task. In order to do so, we add two arguments to the procedure: a list of tasks that must be already terminated at the current time and the current time point. The procedure examines all possible paths until it finds the path that has to start at time zero.

```
      critical_path( Path) :-
        duration( D),                    % see exercise 6(b)
        tasks( Tasks),
        critical_path( Tasks, Path1, D),
        reverse( Path1, Path).           % see exercise 10

      critical_path( [], [], 0).
      critical_path( Tasks, [ T| Path], Time_point) :-
        member( T, Tasks),
        earliest_finish( T, Time_point), % see exercise 6
        task( T, Duration, Tasks1),
        Start is Time_point-Duration,
        critical_path( Tasks1, Path, Start).
```

13.
```
      check_divide( X) :-
        between( N, 1, X),               % see exercise 2 (d)
        between( M, 1, X),
        X is M * N.
```

14.
(a)
```
      increase_price( A, P) :-
        retract( price( A, Pr)),
        NewPr is Pr * (100 + P) / 100,
        assert( price( A, NewPr)).
```
(b)
```
      increase_price( A, P) :-
        retract( price( A, Pr)),
        NewPr is Pr * (100 + P) / 100,
        assert( price( A, NewPr)), fail. % 'fail' is used to
      increase_price( _,_).              % involve backtracking
```

15. It calculates length N of list L.

16.
```
      findall( X, Goals, _) :-
        call( Goals),
        asserta( result( X)),
        fail.                            % return to call( Goals)
      findall( _, _, List) :-            % If call( Goals) does not succeed
        collect( List).                  % collect results (see section 5.3)
                                         % in List.
```

17.
(a)
```
      pickup( X) :-
        not( on( _, X)),
        on( X, _),
        retract( handempty),
        assert( holding( X)),
        retract( on( X, _)).
```
(b)
```
      put( X, Y) :-
        (Y = floor; not( on( _, Y))),
        retract( holding( X)),
        assert( handempty),
        assert( on( X, Y)).
```

(c)   ```
clear(X) :-
  not(on(_, X)).
clear(X) :-
  X \== floor,
  on(Y, X),
  clear(Y), pickup(Y),   % see (a)
  put(Y, floor).   % see (b)
```

18.
```
issue(milk, Litres, fresh, Litres) :-
  state(milk, fresh, L),
  L >= Litres, !,
  issued(milk, fresh, Litres).
issue(milk, Litres, powdered, Kilos) :-
  Kilos is Litres * 0.125,
  issued(milk, powdered, Kilos).
```

19.
```
same_var(bla, Y) :-   % Instantiate the first variable.
  var(Y), !,   % If the second variable is not
  fail.   % also instantiated then fail.
same_var(X, Y) :-   % If the first clause does not
  var(X),   % succeed then check if both
  var(Y).   % variables are uninstantiated.
```

20.
```
write_list([]).
write_list([tab(X)| Tail]) :-
  tab(X),   % built-in procedure
  write_list(Tail).
write_list([nl| Tail]) :-
  nl,
  write_list(Tail).
write_list([X| Tail]) :-
  write(X),
  write_list(Tail).
```

21.
```
copy(Input, Output) :-
  see(Input),
  tell(output),
  copy,
  seen,
  told.
copy :-
  get0(X),
  put(X),
  copy.
copy.   % Succeed when end_of_file is reached.
```
```

22.

```
parent :-
  write( 'Whose parent are you searching for? '),
  read( X),
  child( X, Y),
  write_list( ['The parent of ', X, ' is ', Y]).
 /* see exercise 20 */
```

23.

```
consult1( F, Pred/N) :-
  see( F),
  consult_clause( Pred/N),
  seen.

consult_clause( Pred/N) :-
  read( Clause),
  treat( Clause, Pred, N).

treat( end_of_file, _, _).
treat(( Head :- Body), Pred, N) :-
  functor( Head, Pred, N),
  assertz(( Head :- Body)),
  consult_clause( Pred/N).
treat( Fact, Pred, N) :-
  functor( Fact, Pred, N),           % Fact of the procedure Pred
  assertz( Fact),
  consult_clause( Pred/N).
treat( _, Pred, N) :-                % Clause is not from
  consult_clause( Pred/N).           % procedure Pred.
```

108

Chapter 6

Guidelines for Programming in Prolog

The aims of good Prolog programming, which are a precondition for writing efficient programs, are that the program is correct, readable, efficient, robust with the regard to erroneous data, properly documented, and easy to modify and extend. Using the Prolog debugging facility, program errors can be quickly discovered and removed. Because of its declarative semantics, simple syntax and understandable control strategy, Prolog enables efficient development of programs.

6.1 How to Make Programs More Readable

Solving a certain programming task may take us a great deal of time, say several weeks, months or even years. When programming we must keep in mind that after some time, someone might want to review the code and continue the work therefore the program code must be readable and the program well documented.

We have already encountered some features that make a program more readable. In section 2.2 we pointed out the importance of the layout of programs. We suggested that each goal in the body of a rule is written in a separate line and the body of a rule is indented from the head of a rule. Clauses about the same procedure should be written together and a blank line between procedures makes a program more readable. It is most important that the same stylistic conventions are used throughout the program.

Procedures should be short, containing only few clauses, as long procedures are hard to understand. The only exceptions are tabular procedures containing a set of facts or procedures with a unique structure of clauses.

Using Mnemonic Names

In order to write readable programs we should use mnemonic names, i.e. names that explicitly denote objects and relations that they denote. The name of a procedure should indicate what it actually does, i.e. what operation it performs or what its purpose is. There is an obvious difference between the readability of the program:

```
a( peter, ann).
a( peter, tom).

b( C, D) :-
   a( D, C).
```

and the program:

```
child( peter, ann).
child( peter, tom).

parent( X, Y) :-
   child( Y, X).
```

Mnemonic names of variables explain the meaning of procedure's arguments. In the above program it is not obvious which argument stands for a parent and which for a child. By using mnemonic names we obtain a more readable program:

```
parent( Parent, Child) :-
   child( Child, Parent).
```

In order to make structures more readable, it is sometimes useful to replace constants with simple structures. Suppose we have facts in a form

```
'bill( Bill_number, Cashiers_number, Shop_code, Amount).'
```

It is impossible to understand what is the meaning of the following fact:

```
bill( 171, 21, 143, 1510).
```

To avoid this weakness we may replace every constant by a simple structure, such as:

```
bill( no( 171), cashier( 21), shop( 143), amount( 1510)).
```

Avoiding Disjunctions

Clauses that use both conjunctions and disjunctions of goals are difficult to understand. We can overcome this problem by splitting one clause into several clauses in order to get rid of disjunctions. In section 2.2 we have defined a 'grandmother' relation with the following procedure:

```
grandmother( X, Y) :-
   mother( X, Z),
   (mother( Z, Y);
    father( Z, Y)).
```

We can split the rule into two clauses:

```
grandmother( X, Y) :-
   mother( X, Z),
   mother( Z, Y).
grandmother( X, Y) :-
   mother( X, Z),
   father( Z, Y).
```

110

Such splitting is made at the expense of the length of a program and its efficiency. A better way to overcome this problem is by introducing a new predicate which is then defined separately:

```
grandmother( X, Y) :-
   mother( X, Z),
   parent( Z, Y).

parent( X, Y) :-
   mother( X, Y);
   father( X, Y).
```

Affecting the Declarative Meaning by the Use of 'Cut'

When using cut we should try not to change the declarative meaning of procedures, i.e. 'green cuts' are prefered to 'red cuts'. If this is not possible we should use comments to explain the procedural meaning of a clause containing the 'red cut'. For example, in section 5.4 we had a procedure for computing the maximal element of a list of numbers. To avoid the redundant computations we have used cut. Comments explain the meaning of the program:

```
max( 0, []).               % when a list is empty
max( X, [ X]).
max( M, [ X| Tail]) :-
   max( M, Tail),          % If the maximal element is in the
   X =< M, !.              % tail this is the only solution.
max( X, [ X| _]).          % If the third clause does not
                           % succeed, the maximal element is
                           % in the head of s list.
```

Although cut affects the declarative meaning of a program, it can be used to implement some useful and clearly defined constructs such as the 'if-then-else' construct for selecting between the alternatives. Suppose we have the following example:

```
if Cond
then Goal1
else Goal2
```

We may implement this construct by defining the procedure 'if-then-else(Cond, Goal1, Goal2)' in the following way:

```
if_then_else( Cond, Goal1, _) :-
   call( Cond), !,
   call( Goal1).
if_then_else( _, _, Goal2) :-
   call( Goal2).
```

Using this procedure we can solve the problem of searching a maximal element of a list by:

```
max( 0, []).
max( X, [ X]).
max( M, [ X| Tail]) :-
   max( M1, Tail),
   if_then_else( X =< M1, M = M1, M = X).
```

111

A Careful Use of 'assert' and 'retract'

In section 5.3 we introduced the built-in procedures 'assert' and 'retract'. We have pointed out that both procedures should be used with care since they enable changing the program during its execution. Sometimes this feature may be extremely useful, although it definitely affects the transparency of the program's behaviour and therefore also its understandability. We should try to restrict the use of the procedures 'assert' and 'retract' to save and restore temporal results only. In any case, the use of procedures 'assert' and 'retract' should be thoroughly commented.

Exercises

1. Try to eliminate the ambiguity in the following facts (which semantically represent different relations, although they use the same predicate):
(a) `child( jane, ann).`
(b) `child( [jane, peter], ann).`
(c) `child( ann, 2).`

2. Try to make the following rules more readable:
```
(a)  likes( Teacher, Pupil):-
         diligent( Pupil);
         naughty( Pupil),
         bright(Pupil).
(b) way_home( Office, Home) :-
         walk( Office, Station),
         (by_bus( Station, Station1); by_train( Station, Station1)),
         walk( Station1, Home).
```

3. Correct the following program for computing the minimal number of three numbers and make the program more readable.

```
max( X, Y, Z, X) :-
   X > Y,
   X > Z, !.
max( X, Y, Z, Y) :-
   Y > X,
   Y > Z, !.
max( _, _, Z, Z).
```

6.2 Using Operators

In section 3.4 we saw that the infix notation, usually used in mathematics, is more convenient for arithmetic expressions. This notation is much more readable than the standard Prolog prefix notation, in which a functor is followed by arguments, enclosed in brackets and separated by commas. In general, infix notation in Prolog is made possible by the use of *operators*.

In arithmetic expressions, we use the following built-in infix operators:

' + ', ' − ', '*', '/', 'div' and 'mod'

Evaluation of arithmetic expressions can be performed by built-in predicates, also defined as infix operators:

'is', '>', '<', '>=', '=<', '=:=' and '=\='.

Generally, the user can define his own operators so that, for example, the following expressions become regular Prolog terms:

```
A & B  v C => D
if X then Y else Z
ann is_a mother of tom
```

Operators may be *unary* or *binary*, having one or two arguments, respectively. Unary operators may be defined as *prefix*, which is appropriate, for example, in the following cases:

```
if X                        % condition X
~ X                         % negation of X
- X                         % minus X
?- X                        % goal X in a query
```

or *postfix* as, for example, in the case of:

```
X.                          % a period
```

Binary operators are defined as *infix*, for example:

```
A & B                       % conjunction
A \ B                       % set difference
A is_a B                    % relation 'is_a'
A :- B                      % delimiter of the head and the body of a clause
```

When using operators, brackets are omitted which may lead to ambiguity if there are several operators in one expression. The *precedence* of operators is used to avoid this ambiguity. It determines how strongly an operator binds its arguments. Precedence is an integer number between 1 and 1200 (this range depends on the particular implementation). The lower the precedence of the operator, the stronger the operator binds its arguments. The precedence enables to interpret terms with different operators, for example:

a + b * c   is equivalent to   a + (b * c),

since '*' binds stronger than ' + ', i.e. the precedence of '*' is lower than the precedence of ' + '.

We already know that each Prolog structure may be represented in the form of a tree. The tree representation of the above arithmetic expression is given in Figure 6.1. Note that the operator with the highest precedence is the root of the tree. We may define the precedence of a term as the precedence of its principal functor, i.e. the operator that is in the root of the tree representing this structure. Therefore, the precedence of the term 'a + b * c' is equal to the precedence of the operator ' + '.

113

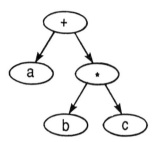

Figure 6.1   The tree representation of the expression 'a + b * c'.

A simple term and a term enclosed in brackets have precedence 0. Therefore the precedence of the term '(a + b) * c' equals the precedence of the operator '*'.

The *associativity* of an operator determines how to interpret terms with more than one operator of the same precedence. An operator may be *left associative*, meaning that the leftmost instance of the operator binds stronger than other instances. For example:

a + b + c + d = ((a + b) + c) + d

If we define the operator '&' to be *right associative*, then the following two terms are equal:

a & b & c & d = a & (b & (c & d))

An operator may also be without associativity. This means that at most one operator with the same precedence may appear in a single term without brackets. For example:

a :- b :- c

is an invalid term, while the terms:

(a :- b) :- c and a :- (b :- c)

are valid since the operator ':-' has no associativity.

The *type* of an operator determines whether the operator is prefix, postfix or infix. It also determines the operator's associativity. The valid operator types are given in Figure 6.2. The symbol 'f' stands for the operator, 'x' for an argument, whose precedence is strictly lower than that of the operator, and 'y' stands for the argument with a lower or equal precedence.

type	meaning	arity	associativity
fx	prefix	unary	no
fy	prefix	unary	right
xf	postfix	unary	no
yf	postfix	unary	left
xfx	infix	binary	no
yfx	infix	binary	left
xfy	infix	binary	right

Figure 6.2   The valid types of Prolog operators.

Each operator is defined by its precedence, type and name. A user may define his own operators using a command of the following form:

:- op(Precedence, Type, Name).

Syntactically, the name of an operator must be an atom such as '*', ' + ', '&', 'v', ' = >', 'if', 'is__a', etc. The 'standard' Prolog built-in operators are given in Appendix B.

Assume that we have a program for manipulating logic expressions. In this program we want to write a logic expression in the same way as in mathematical logic:

~A & B v C = > D

We have to define the three operators ' = >', '&' and 'v' in the infix notation. We can do this by the following commands:

```
:- op( 90, fy, ~).          % negation
:- op( 100, xfy, &).        % conjunction
:- op( 110, xfy, v).        % disjunction
:- op( 120, xfx, '=>').     % implication
```

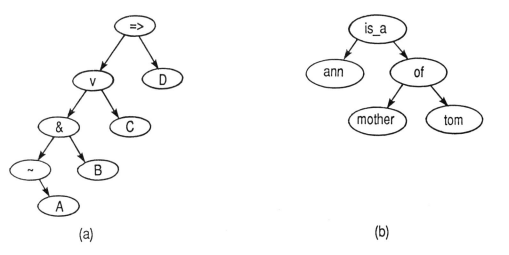

(a)

(b)

Figure 6.3   The tree representations of terms ' ~A & B v C = > D' and 'ann is__a mother of tom'.

115

The structure of the term is illustrated in Figure 6.3 (a). The operators used to construct the term 'ann is__a mother of tom' are defined as:

```
:- op( 151, xfx, is_a).
:- op( 150, xfx, of).
```

The structure of the term is illustrated in Figure 6.3 (b).

Exercises

4. Define operators that will make the following terms valid Prolog structures:
(a) if X then Y else Z
(b) Y would__like X if X were good and X were bright.

5. Write the following expressions as the standard Prolog structures:
(a) ~A & B v C => D
(b) if X then Y else Z
(c) ann is__a mother of tom

6. Suppose we have the following definitions of operators:
```
:- op( 700, xfx, \\).
:- op( 600, xfx, //).
:- op( 600, xfy, ':').
:- op( 400, yfx, to).
:- op( 400, xfx, from).
```
Draw trees that represent the structures:
(a) Flight // Number from From to To \\ Day : Hours : Minutes
(b) 1 from A to C : 2 from B to C : 3 from A to B

7. (*) Write the interpreters of clauses in exercise 4.

6.3 Top-down Approach to Prolog Programming

Decomposition of a Problem

A useful technique for solving complex problems is to try to identity reasonable sub-problems and solve them separately. The original problem can usually be replaced by several simpler problems which are easier to solve. Suppose that we have a problem P that can be split into three sub-problems P1, P2 and P3. Each sub-problem can be further split into other sub-problems. Such a decomposition of a problem is illustrated in Figure 6.4:

This decomposition of a problem may be directly encoded in Prolog:

```
p :- p1, p2, p3.
p1 :- p11, p12.
p3 :- p31, p32, p33.
```

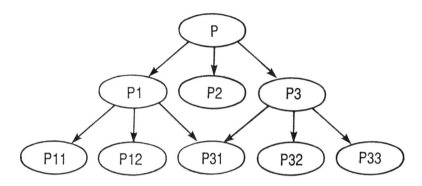

Figure 6.4 A hierarchical decomposition of a problem into sub-problems.

The sub-problem P2 could be solved by a special procedure or again by decomposing it into sub-problems. The Prolog syntax itself encourages us to partition the problem in this *top-down* manner. The first clause above directly states that we can solve P by solving P1, P2 and P3. The *main procedure* of the program which solves the entire problem, is usually written at the top of the program and utility procedures are at the bottom.

A particular sub-problem is usually solved by a separate program, sometimes called a *module*. A module is a set of procedures saved in a separate file. It solves a particular problem or a certain type of problems. The main module of the entire program controls the execution of the program by consulting particular modules and transferring the execution to the programs they consist of.

Typically, the main module contains a command for consulting the modules that constitute the program, for example:

```
:- ( [file_p11, file_p12, file_p2, file_p31, file_p32, file_p33].
```

Therefore, the command for consulting the main module:

```
:- consult( main).
```

will invoke consultation of all the files, one after another.

Decomposition of Data Structures

Efficient solutions to problems depend greatly on the choice of data structures. One should devote enough attention to finding suitable data structures, as the same information may be represented in many different ways which may strongly affect the simplicity, clarity and efficiency.

It is useful to decompose data structures in a top-down manner in order to be able to deal with different levels of detail. To illustrate the top-down approach we represent the example of storing personal data (also given as a sample in section 3.2) of the form:

117

```
person( name( Name, Fam_name), address( Place, Street, Number),
        birth( Place_of_birth, date( Day, Month, Year)))
```

on Figure 6.5.

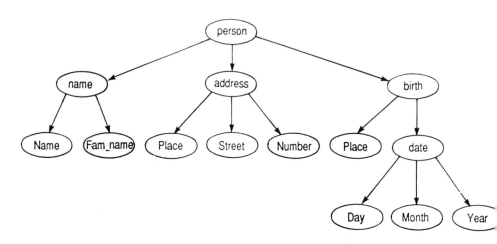

Figure 6.5   A top-down specification of personal data.

The same data could be represented by the structures given in figure 6.6. These structures are, obviously, less appropriate, as related sub-structures are not grouped together.

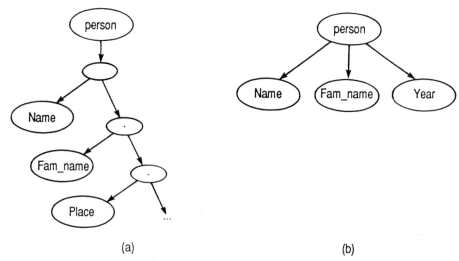

(a)   (b)

Figure 6.6   The tree representations of structures
(a) person([Name, Fam__name, Place, Street, Number, Place__of__birth, Day, Month, Year]), and
(b) person(Name, Fam__name, Place, Street, Number, Place__of__birth, Day, Month, Year)

118

Exercises

3. Figure 6.7 suggests a possible decomposition of the problem of solving linear equations with one unknown into subproblems. Write the corresponding Prolog code.

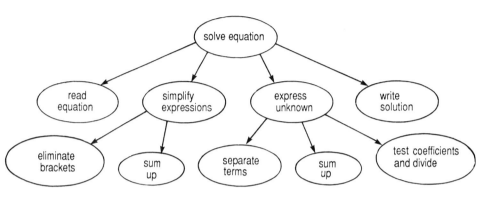

Figure 6.7 Decomposition of the problem of solving linear equations with one unknown.

9. Which of the structures is better?

a) (a1) patient(Name, Age, Room, Diagnosis) or
   (a2) patient(name(Name, Age), room(Room, Diagnosis))
b) (b1) week([mon, tue, wen, thu, fri sat, sun]) or
   (b2) week(beg([mon, tue]),
              mid([wen, thu]),
              end([fri sat, sun]))
c) (c1) paper([Title, Authors, Abstract, Keywords, Introd,
              Chap1, Chap2, Chap3, Chap4, Concl, Acknowledge,
              Refer, Appendix1, Appendix2]) or
   (c2) paper(first_page([Title, Authors, Abstract, Keywords]),
              introd(Introd),
              contents([Chap1, Chap2, Chap3, Chap4]),
              conclusions([Concl, Acknowledge]),
              refer(Refer),
              appendices([Appendix1, Appendix2]))

6.4 Efficiency

The advantage of Prolog is that in principle a programmer does not have to bother about how a program is being executed. In practice, especially when writing complex programs, the issue of efficiency and procedural correctness becomes important. The efficiency of a Prolog program is measured by three criteria: the main being the number of matches performed and attempted in the course of a computation which is related to the execution time; the second is the depth of recursion which is limited by some maximal depth (if this is exceeded, the execution is aborted since there is no more memory space available); and the third is the number of generated data structures.

The above criteria may be used for evaluating Prolog programs. In this section we present some programming techniques and tricks which may improve the efficiency of programs.

Using 'Cut'

The cut can be used in order to avoid unnecessary backtracking, so substantially reducing the search space of inferences by pruning the search tree. Using cut, we may obtain a version of the procedure 'member' (introduced in section 5.4) that will find only one solution:

```
member1( X, [ X| _]) :- !.
member1( X, [ _| Tail]) :-
   member1( X, Tail).
```

When searching for other solutions (requested by typing ';') the cut prevents activation of the second clause, so that all alternative solutions are discarded. Both the execution time and the needed memory space are reduced as Prolog does not have to save the execution trace inside the procedure 'member1' (this trace is needed only for possible backtracking).

With the use of the cut, redundant computations may also be prevented. We have already shown two examples of using the cut to avoid recomputation of already computed values in section 5.4. These were the procedure 'max' for searching for a maximal element of a list (in the section discussing the effects of the cut on the declarative meaning of programs) and the procedure 'issue' for issuing milk from a hotel storage (in exercise 18).

Note that the use of the cut may help us also to implement some procedural constructs that are useful for improving efficiency although they do not conform to the standard Prolog philosophy (such as the 'if-then-else' control construct from section 6.1).

The Order of Clauses and Goals

The efficiency can often be improved by choosing the right order of clauses. The simple rule is to place the clauses which are more likely to succeed at the beginning of a procedure. Using this idea we have already improved the efficiency of the procedure 'max' for searching a maximal number in a list in section 5.4, for it is more likely that the maximal element is in the tail than in the head of the list. We have used the same principle in the procedure 'issue' in section 4.3, exercise 16 (see also section 5.4, exercise 18), where the first clause covered the issue of fresh milk, which is the most common case.

The ordering of goals within a clause also affects efficiency. The procedure 'offspring' is inefficient if defined by the following clauses:

```
offspring( X, Y) :-
   child( X, Y).
offspring( X, Y) :-
   offspring( X, Z),
   child( Z, Y).
```

This procedure exhaustively searches a knowledge-base, as it does not take into account that one of the arguments is usually known and that search should start from the known

120

argument. If we reverse the order of goals in the second clause, the problem is solved more efficiently when ancestor Y is known. If we want to have an efficient procedure in case when at least one argument is known, we have to define a separate clause for each case. We may determine which is the input argument using one of the built-in metalogical procedures 'var/1', 'nonvar/1', 'atom/1' or 'atomic/1' (see Appendix A for more details). In our example we use the procedure 'atom/1' and obtain the following program:

```
offspring( X, Y) :-
    child( X, Y).
offspring( X, Y) :-
    atom( Y), !,
    child( Z, Y),
    offspring( X, Z),
offspring( X, Y) :-
    child( X, Z),
    offspring( Z, Y).
```

If ancestor Y is given as an input argument, the second clause will be used. Otherwise, the third clause will be used when executing the procedure.

Storing Derived Facts

The procedure 'assert/1' may be used to save the facts derived by a certain procedure. For example, storing the results of computation may be used to prevent the recomputation of the same results later on. We have already shown an example of such a procedure, namely the procedure 'not__prime' from section 5.3:

```
not_prime( X) :-
    check_divide( X),              % see    section 5.3, exercise 13
    asserta( not_prime( X)).
```

We may also wish to assert negative facts. If we already know that the procedure will fail for certain values, we can force it to fail immediately. This can be achieved by adding 'negative facts' at the beginning of the procedure. Below is an illustration how this can be done by adding a special clause to the procedure 'not__prime' as follows:

```
not_prime( X) :-
    check_divide( X),
    asserta( not_prime( X)).
not_prime( X) :-
    asserta(( not_prime( X) :- !, fail)),
    fail.
```

If, for example, the value of X is 26 which is not a prime number, the fact 'not__prime(26)' is added to the top of the procedure by 'asserta'. If X is instantiated to a prime number, for example 23, the last clause of the procedure is invoked and the clause:

```
not_prime( 23) :- !, fail.
```

is added to the top of the procedure. When testing whether 23 is not a prime, this clause will be matched before 'check__divide' is invoked, and the procedure will fail immediately. Note that such a use of 'assert' is against the rules of 'good' Prolog programming, as it in fact modifies the program and causes the program to be executed differently in different runs Still, when efficiency is most important, such programming tricks are allowed.

Using 'repeat-fail' Loops in Order to Avoid Recursion

Recursive programs require a lot of memory space, since Prolog saves the execution trail fo: the purpose of possible backtracking. We can partially eliminate this problem by using cut A more useful solution is the use of 'repeat', which always succeeds. It is defined by the following procedure:

```
repeat.
repeat :- repeat.
```

The procedure 'copy' from section 5.5 can be rewritten by using 'repeat' as follows:

```
copy :-
  repeat,
  copy_char.

copy_char :-
  get0( Ch), !,
  put( Ch),
  fail.
copy_char.
```

Because of 'fail' and 'repeat', the goals 'get0(Ch)' and 'put(Ch)' are successively resatisfiec until 'end__of__file' is reached. When the goal 'get0(Ch)' fails, the second clause of the procedure 'copy__char' is used to terminate the 'repeat' loop.

For illustration, let us also rewrite the procedure 'do' from section 5.5. Commands ar« executed successively until 'stop' is input:

```
do :-
  repeat,
  write( 'command : '),
  read( Command),
  perform( Command).

perform( stop) :- !.
perform( Command) :-
  execute( Command), !,
  fail.
```

Note that the use of repeat can help us implement the 'repeat-until' control construct familiar from procedural languages.

```
repeat_until( Q, P) :-
  repeat,
  call( ( Q, !)),
  call( P), !.
```

or arbitrary goals P and Q the procedure 'repeat_until(Q, P)' is interpreted as 'repeat Q until P is true'. If P is not satisfied, the goal 'call(P)' fails and 'call((Q, !))' is invoked again. Cut is used to eliminate alternative solutions. Using this construct, the 'do' procedure may be rewritten much more clearly as:

```
do :- repeat_until( do( Command), Command == stop).

do( Command) :-
  write( 'command : '),
  read( Command),
  perform( Command).


perform( stop).
perform( Command) :-
  execute( Command).
```

As the use of 'repeat-fail' loops usually decreases the clarity of programs, it is useful to define such a procedural construct explicitly and use it consistently throughout the program in order to improve its readability.

Note that when using the 'repeat-fail' loop, we can not store intermediate results through variables (we must use 'assert' and 'retract').

Improving the Efficiency of List Concatenation

In section 5.2 the following procedure for list concatenation was introduced:

```
conc( [], L, L).
conc( [ X| L1], L2, [ X| L3]) :-
  conc( L1, L2, L3).
```

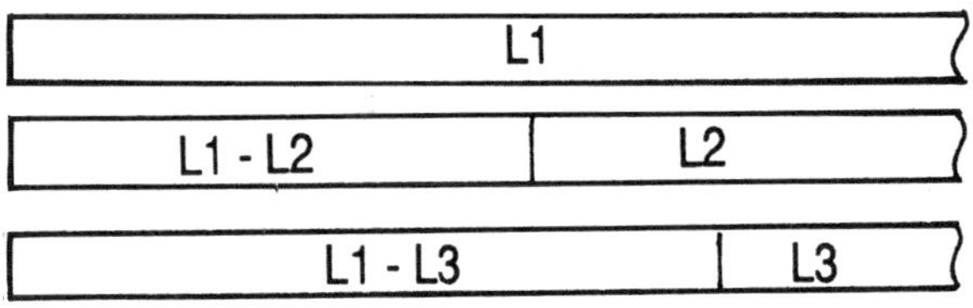

Figure 6.8 Concatenation of lists using the difference-list notation.

This procedure is inefficient for long lists, since the right end of the list in the first argument is difficult to reach. The efficiency of the procedure may be improved by using the *difference list* notation. In this notation, a list ' [a,b,c]' can be represented in any of the following ways

```
[a,b,c]-[], [a,b,c,d]-[d], [a,b,c,d,e]-[d,e], [a,b,c|X]-X
```

The last form is the most general and enables direct access to the right end of the list.

The method of concatenating two lists in a difference-list notation is illustrated in Figure 6.8 The concatenation may be achieved by a single fact (see also exercise 7 in section 4.2):

```
concat ( L1 - L2 - L3, L1 - L3 ).
```

Using the difference-list notation the procedure 'reverse(List, Reversed)' from section 5.2 exercise 10 can be implemented more efficiently by omitting the concatenation operation:

```
reverse( L, R) :-
  reverse1( L, R-[]).

reverse1( [], X-X).                    % empty list
reverse1( [ H| Tail], List-Dif) :-
  reverse1( Tail, List-[ H| Dif]).
```

Prolog Programming Style

The reader may already have noticed that improvement in efficiency may be (and usually is) obtained at the cost of transparency.

Two extreme ways of writing Prolog programs can be identified. The first is to write programs in 'pure' Prolog without using any metalogical and control procedures and not taking into account the efficiency of execution. Such programming enables fast development of correct but inefficient programs. On the other hand, in the procedural way of programming much effort is devoted to the efficiency of programs. In this case, programming is often slower and more erroneous. The resulting programs are usually hard to understand and are similar to programs written in procedural languages.

The suggested solution is to appropriately determine the trade-off between the transparency and the efficiency of a particular program and find a compromise between the two extremes. In each case, special programming techniques and tricks that make it possible to write more efficient programs should be thoroughly commented.

Note

Improving the efficiency of a procedure usually affects its use, i.e. affects the non-determinism involving the choice of possible input and output arguments. For example, the procedure 'member1' defined by using cut cannot be used for accessing an arbitrary element of a list: the procedure 'concat', using the difference-list notation, cannot be used for splitting a list into two sublists; the use of metalogical procedures 'var/1', 'nonvar/1', 'atom/1' and 'atomic/1' requires additional clauses to make procedures usable in different directions.

Exercises

10. When executing the procedure 'offspring' defined in this section, the goal 'atom(Y)' for ancestor Y is tested in every recursive call of the procedure. Try to overcome this weakness.

1. How can the empty list be represented in the difference-list notation?

2. (*) The quicksort algorithm for sorting a list of numbers is the following:
   1. Take the first element of a list.
   2. Split the tail of the list into two sublists: the first containing numbers that are greater than the first element of the list and the second containing numbers that are smaller than or equal to the first element.
   3. Sort recursively each of the sublists.
   4. Concatenate both sublists inserting the original first element between them.

   (a) Write the procedure for 'quicksort'.
   (b) Increase the efficiency of the procedure by using the difference-list notation.

6.5 Debugging

Debugging means searching and removing errors from a program. Syntactic errors are detected by the Prolog interpreter itself. However, a missing letter in the name of a procedure or of a constant is not a syntactic error but is interpreted as the definition of a new procedure or the use of a new constant. If a variable is used in a clause only once (and is not an anonymous variable) this is usually an error and some Prolog interpreters return a message about such occurences.

It is more difficult to detect semantic mistakes that stem from insufficient understanding of the problem or of the solution run. These errors may be detected only from the incorrect execution of the program, usually apparent from the wrong input/output behaviour of a procedure. In this case the critical task is to find the erroneous procedure. If a procedure gives wrong answers, then either the procedure is incorrect or the procedures invoked by procedure calls (i.e. goals) in bodies of clauses are wrong. A straightforward method for discovering an incorrect part of a program is to follow its execution trace until incorrect behaviour is detected. This is provided by the Prolog trace facility. Compared to procedural languages, detecting errors in Prolog is substantially easier because of the simple control of the execution of Prolog programs.

Introducing the Box Model of Debugging

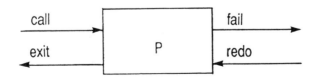

Figure 6.9   The box representation of the procedure P.

The execution of each Prolog procedure may be viewed as a box with four ports: two entries ('call' and 'redo') and two exits ('exit' and 'fail'), as shown in Figure 6.9. When a procedure is invoked for the first time, the execution is started at the 'call' entry. If the execution fails it exits through the 'fail' port, and if it successfully finds a solution it ends through 'exit'. If through backtracking the execution returns to the same procedure the 'redo' entry is used.

Let us consider the 'weather' program given in section 4.1 execution of which was discussed in section 4.3.

```
nice :-
  warm.
nice :-
  sunny,
  not_windy.

warm :-
  temperature( T),
  T > 20.
not_windy :-
  wind_speed( S),
  S < 5.

sunny.
temperature( 15).
wind_speed( 3).
```

The box representation of the execution of this procedure is given in Figure 6.10.

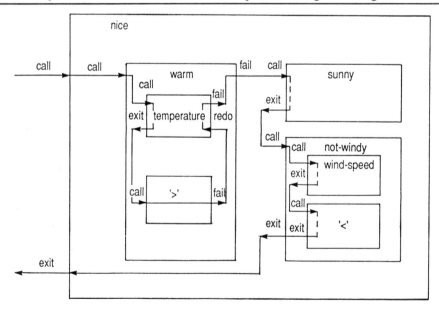

Figure 6.10 Execution of the procedure 'weather'.

Procedures 'trace' and 'notrace'

In order to trace the execution of a program we can use the built-in procedures 'trace' to switch the tracing mode on and 'notrace' to switch it off. When the tracing mode is on, Prolog displays every execution step that goes through any port of a procedure (talking in terms of the box representation introduced above).

Let us illustrate the execution trace of the procedure 'weather' as displayed when the tracing mode is on.

```
?- trace.                      % This command switches the trace on.
yes                            % 'trace' succeeds.
?- nice.                       % Can the goal 'nice' be satisfied?
call> nice
  call> warm
    call> temperature(T)
    exit< temperature(15)
    call> 15 > 20
    fail< 15 > 20
    redo> temperature(T)
    fail< temperature(T)
  fail< warm
  call> sunny
  exit< sunny
  call> not_windy
    call> wind_speed(S)
    exit< wind_speed(3)
    call> 3 < 5
    exit< 3 < 5
  exit< not_windy
exit< nice
yes
```

At the end of each displayed line 'return' was pressed to continue the step by step tracing of the execution. Of course, for longer programs this may be very cumbersome. The majority of Prolog implementations allow entering an appropriate command (instead of 'return') which causes skipping parts of the execution trace. Such commands either continue the execution without tracing, disable tracing until the 'exit' port of the current procedure is reached, immediately fail the procedure call or abort the execution.

Sometimes it is useful to trace only particular procedures by skipping the ones that are presumably correct. Typically, we will always skip the execution trace for all utility procedures that have already been thoroughly tested. The built-in procedure 'spy/1' is used to select the procedure to be traced. The procedure 'spy(Procedure)' will invoke the tracing mode only when passing the 'call' port of the given procedure.

The tracing mechanism is a fast way of detecting incorrect behaviour of procedures. When developing a program it is useful to test every new procedure separately as soon as it is typed in. This enables effective development of large programs. Writing new procedures and concatenating them with the existing part of a program is efficient as all procedures have previously been tested for correctness.

6.6 Documentation

Every program should be appropriately documented. We distinguish between the user's and the programmer's documentation. The documentation for the user should suffice for the correct usage of the program. The programmer's documentation should enable understanding, correcting, changing and expanding the program.

Basic documentation consists of the listing of a program with all the necessary comments. Comments should be written while programming if we want them to be correct and written without additional effort. If comments are included after the program is already written it is very likely that some comments are wrong. Wrong comments are much worse than no comments at all. Comments should include the purpose and usage of procedures, description and meaning of input/output arguments, limits on the usage of procedures and explanation of difficult or opaque parts of the code.

A user's guide contains instructions to how the program is to be used, what are the possible errors when using the program, the expected computer time for running the program, the memory limitations and possible compatibility requirements.

A programmer's guide explains implementational features, includes the description of a program's task, methods and algorithms as well as the outline of the structure of the entire program and its data structures. It has to be written at a level of detail which enables understanding, correcting, changing and expanding the program.

6.7 Summary

−A good program is correct, transparent, efficient, robust well documented and thus easy to modify and extend.

−The program's transparency may be improved by using mnemonic names of variables, constants, functors and procedures. The layout of a program is also very important and should be consistent throughout the program.

−Metalogical and control procedures such as 'cut', 'assert' and 'retract' should be carefully used and commented. Preferably they should not decrease transparency by affecting the declarative meaning of a program.

−Using disjunctions may harm the transparency of a program. You can overcome this problem by splitting a clause into several clauses or by introducing new procedures.

−Operators improve readability. Operators may be unary (prefix or postfix) or binary (infix). They may have either left or right associativity or no associativity at all. The precedence of an operator determines how strong an operator binds its arguments.

−In the top-down development of programs the problem is split into subproblems that are easier to solve. Prolog supports this programming style as it does not require the declaration of variables at the beginning of a program. It enables structures to be further extended and elaborated in procedures on lower (later) levels of program development.

–Efficiency can be improved by using the cut to prevent unnecessary backtracking or redundant computation of results that are already computed. 'assert' may be used to store results that are frequently needed. 'repeat' is used for repetitive execution of the same operations in order to save the memory space, required when solving the same problem with a recursive program.

–An appropriate ordering of clauses and goals may improve efficiency. Additional clauses may be introduced for different use of input/output arguments of a procedure.

–A difference-list notation enables effective access to the right end of a list.

–Using the Prolog debugging facility, program errors may be quickly discovered and removed. A box representation is used to trace the execution of Prolog programs. The built-in procedures 'trace/0' and 'spy/1' control the tracing of the execution.

–Program documentation includes a listing of the code, a user's guide and a programmer's guide. The code has to be thoroughly commented.

6.8 Solutions to Exercises

1.
(a) `child( jane, ann).`
(b) `children( [jane, peter], ann).`
(c) `number_of_children( ann, 2).`

2.
(a)
```
likes( Teacher, Pupil) :-
    diligent( Pupil).
likes( Teacher, Pupil) :-
    naughty( Pupil),
    bright( Pupil).
```

(b)
```
way_home( Office, Home) :-
    walk( Office, Station),
    travel( Station, Station1),
    walk( Station1, Home).

travel( Station, Station1) :-
    by_bus( Station, Station1);
    by_train( Station, Station1).
```

(c)
```
win_a_boxing_match( X, Y) :-
    knock_out( X, Y), !.
win_a_boxing_match( X, Y) :-
    points( X, Px),
    points( Y, Py),
    Px > Py.
```

3.  ```
    max( X, Y, Z, X) :-
        X >= Y,
        X >= Z.
    max( X, Y, Z, Y).
        Y >= X,
        Y >= Z.
    max( X, Y, Z, Z) :-
        Z >= X,
        Z >= Y.
    ```

4.
(a) ```
     :- op(500, xfx, then).
     :- op(400, fx, if).
     :- op(400, xfx, else).
     ```
(b)  ```
     :- op( 500, xfx, would_like).
     :- op( 1000, xfx, if).
     :- op( 300, xfx, were).
     :- op( 400, xfy, and).
     ```

5.
(a) `=>(V(&(~(A), B), C), D)`
(b) `then( if( X), else( Y, Z))`
(c) `is_a( ann, of( mother, tom))`

6. See Figure 6.11.

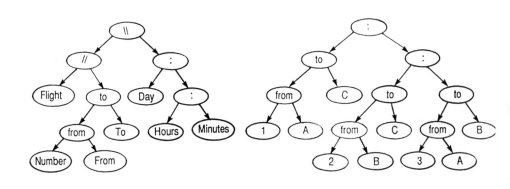

Figure 6.11 Solutions to exercise 6.

7.
(a) ```
     if X then Y else _ :- call(X), !, call(Y).
     if _ then _ else Z̄ :- call(Z).
     ```

130

(b) ```
Conclusion if Condition :- satisfy(Condition).
satisfy(A and B) :- satisfy(A), satisfy(B).
satisfy(X were Y) :- P =.. [Y, X], call(P).
```

8. ```
solve_eq :-
    read_eq( Eg),
    simplify_ex( Eg, Eg1),
    express_unk( Eg1, Solution),
    write_sol( Solution).

simplify_ex( Eg, Eg1) :-
    elim_brackets( Eg, NewEg),
    sum_up( NewEg, Eg1).

express_unk( Eg, Solution) :-
    separate_terms( Eg, Eg1),
    sum_up( Eg1, Eg2),
    test_divide( Eg2,Solution).
```

9.
(a) (a1) as arguments can not be grouped in a meaningful way
(b) (b1) the grouping in (b2) makes no sense
(c) (c2) the grouping of arguments makes sense; the 'contents' may be expanded to include arbitrarily many chapters.

10. You can define a separate procedure for each case.
```
offspring( X, Y) :-
    atom( Y), !,
    offspring1( X, Y).
offspring( X, Y) :-
    offspring2( X, Y).

offspring1( X, Y) :-
    child( X, Y).
offspring1( X, Y) :-
    child( Z, Y),
    offspring1( X, Z).

offspring2( X, Y) :-
    child( X, Y).
offspring2( X, Y) :-
    child( X, Z),
    offspring2( Z, Y).
```

11. X-X

12.
(a) ```
quicksort([X], [X]).
quicksort([X| Tail], Sorted) :-
    split(X, Tail, T1, T2),
    quicksort(T1, S1),
    quicksort(T2, S2),
    conc(S1, [X| S2], Sorted).
```
```

```
    split( _, [], [], []).
    split( X̄, [ Y| Tail], [ Y| S], G) :-
        Y > X, !,
      split( X, Tail, S, G).
    split( X, [ Y| Tail], S, [ Y| G]) :-
        Y =< X,
      split( X, Tail, S, G).

(b) quicksort( List, Sorted) :-
      quicksort1( List, Sorted-[]).

    quicksort1( [], X-X).
    quicksort1( [ X| Tail], Sorted-Dif) :-
      split( X, Tail, T1, T2),          % see (a)
      quicksort1( T1, Sorted-[ X| Dif1]),
      quicksort1( T2, Dif1-Dif).

    /* The last two goals implicitly perform the concatenation.
       The same could be achieved by using the procedure 'concat'
       from section 6.4 with the goal
       'concat( Sorted-[ X| Dif1], Dif1-Dif, Sorted-Dif)' */
```

Chapter 7

Prolog Programs for Various Problem Domains

Prolog is a powerful programming tool for the quick development of programs, because of its flexible data structures and because the types of variables do not have to be specified. On the other hand, Prolog is not appropriate for programming applications that consume a lot of time and memory space, at least for today's computer configurations. It is also not appropriate for numerical computations, as it does not enable direct access and changing the values of variables.

In this chapter the emphasis is on exercises. Only the most basic principles are explained, while the reader is encouraged to solve particular problems through a series of graded exercises. Although opposed to the 'top-down' approach to problem solving advertised before, exercises are designed to lead the reader from solutions of sub-problems to solutions of more complex problems. The solutions at the end of the chapter are explained in detail.

7.1 Data Structures Manipulation

The most frequently used data structures are lists, trees and graphs. Note that lists are a special case of trees and trees a special case of graphs. Since lists and trees are defined recursively, most of the operations on lists and trees are defined recursively as well.

Each Prolog structure may be represented in the form of a tree, so lists and trees are encoded in Prolog directly. Lists can be used to represent sets and even arrays, although arrays are rarely used in Prolog programming. In lists, direct access to each element is not possible, which limits the usefulness of so represented arrays. For example, a two dimensional array is represented by a list of lists. To access an arbitrary element of such an array (in row I and coloumn J), the following procedure may be used:

```
access( I, J, Array, X) :-          % X is the required element
   s=,, [str|Array], arg( I, S, Row),   % arg is a built-in procedure
   S1=,, [str1|Row], arg( J, S1, X).
```

133

The problem of how to change the value of such an element still remains unsolved.

Graphs can not be represented directly. Usually they are represented by a set of facts determining the edges or by the list of edges between the nodes. Graphs may contain cycles, therefore it is useful to record the trail to prevent cycling when searching for a path in a graph as shown in section 5.2.

Exercises

1. Suppose a binary tree is represented by the structure:

```
btree( Element, Left_subtree, Right_subtree)
```

where a subtree is again a binary tree, or 'nil' if empty. A binary tree may also be represented as a list of elements and 'nils', starting with the root element, continuing with the elements of the left subtree and ending with the elements of the right subtree. Define the procedure 'transform(Tree, List)' that will transform a binary tree into a list and vice versa. Here are two examples of its use:

```
?- transform( btree( 1, btree(2,nil,nil), btree(3,nil,nil)), List).
List = [ 1, 2, nil, nil, 3, nil, nil]
yes
?- transform( Tree, [ 1, nil, 2, 3, nil, nil, nil]).
Tree = btree( 1, nil, btree( 2, btree(3, nil, nil), nil))
yes
```

2. A binary dictionary is a tree whose root element is greater than all the elements in the left subtree and smaller than all the elements in the right subtree. Note that a binary dictionary represents a set, i.e. no element appears twice in the dictionary. Define the procedures:

(a) 'in(X, Dict)'– true, if X is in the dictionary
(b) 'add(X, Old__dic, New__dic)'– add X to the dictionary if X is not in it (if X is already in the dictionary, it remains unchanged)
(c) (*) del(X, Old__dic, New__dic) – delete X from the dictionary (if X is not in the dictionary, it remains unchanged)

3. In section 5.2, exercise 11, we defined the procedure 'exists__path(X, Y, Path)' that finds a Path (i.e. a list of nodes) between nodes X and Y in a directed graph given by a set of facts of the form 'arc(X, Y)'. Define the procedure 'min__path(X, Y, Path)' that will return the minimal path from X to Y, i.e. the path with the smallest number of arcs. Use the *breadth-first* strategy: at each step examine all possible paths of a fixed length and then increment the length until node Y is reached (i.e. the minimal path is found), or until all possible paths are exhausted.

7.2 Symbolic Mathematics

The flexibility of its data structures makes Prolog a powerful language for *symbolic programming*. Using arithmetic operators, we can easily solve algebraic problems like symbolic equation solving, symbolic differentiation and symbolic integration.

Here is a program for differentiating arithmetic expressions containing four basic arithmetic operations. Variables U and V denote expressions, X denotes an independent variable and C a constant:

```
d( -U, X, -DU) :- !, d( U, X, DU).
d( U + V, X, DU + DV) :- !, d( U, X, DU), d( V, X, DV).
d( U-V, X, DU - DV) :- !, d( U, X, DU), d( V, X, DV).
d( U * V, X, V * DU + U * DV) :- !, d( U, X, DU), d( V, X, DV).
d( U / V, X, (V * DU - U * DV) / ( V * V)):- !,
    d( U, X, DU), d( V, X, DV).
d( X, X, 1) :- !.
d( C, X, 0) :- !.
```

The next example is from computation theory. A *finite automaton* is the simplest abstract machine that reads a string of symbols and decides whether to accept or to reject it. It is determined by a set of states, with a distinguished initial state and a subset of final states, a set of input symbols (an alphabeth) and a set of transitions between the states under given input characters. The problem is to determine whether the input word is an element of the language accepted by the automaton.

The automaton starts from the initial state. At each step it reads one character of the input word and changes the state, depending on the current input character. When the string of input characters is exhausted, execution stops. If the automaton stops in one of the final states, the input word is accepted, otherwise it is rejected.

A finite automaton can be represented by a directed graph: nodes represent states; arcs labelled with input characters represent transitions between the states under particular input characters; doubly circled nodes represent final states; and a node with an input arc with no label represents the initial state. An example of a finite automaton is given in Figure 7.1.

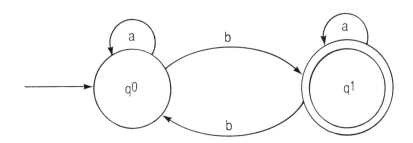

Figure 7.1   A finite automaton.

The automaton in Figure 7.1 has two states, q0 being the initial and q1 the final state. Note that it accepts words of the alphabet {a,b} consisting of an odd number of b characters. In Prolog, the automaton can be defined by the following set of facts:

```
initial( q0).
final( q1).
trans( q0, a, q0).
trans( q0, b, q1).
trans( q1, a, q1).
trans( q1, b, q0).
```

The following procedure defines a simulator of an arbitrary finite automaton. The procedure succeeds if the automaton accepts the input word (given as a list of characters), and fails otherwise.

```
accept( Word) :-
    initial( State),         % start in the initial state
    accept( State, Word).

accept( State, []) :-        % in case of an empty input word
    final( State).           % accept if in the final state
accept( State, [ X| Word]) :-
    trans( State, X, State1),
    accept( State1, Word).
```

We may then have the following dialogue:

```
?- accept( [ a, b, b, a]).
no
?- accept( [ a, b, a, b, a, a, b]).
yes
```

Exercises

4. Extend the procedure for symbolic differentiation to handle arithmetic expression containing the power function X^C (X to the power of C), exponentiation exp(X) trigonometric functions sin(X), cos(X), tan(X) and logarithm ln(X). The differentiation rules are given below. U denotes an expression and C a constant.

```
d( U^0) = 0
d( U^C) = C * U^( C-1) * d( U), for C =\= 0
d( exp( U)) = exp( U) * d( U)
d( sin( U)) = cos( U) * d( U)
d( cos( U)) =-sin( U) * d( U)
d( tan( U)) = 1 / ( cos( U)^2) * d( U)
d( ln( U)) = 1 / U * d( U)
```

5. (*) An extension of finite automata are non-deterministic finite automata with empt transitions. An automaton is non-deterministic if more than one transition from a stat under a certain input character is possible. Empty transitions occur independently of inpu and the input word does not change.

Modify the procedure from section 7.2 to define a simulator of a non-deterministic finite automaton with empty transitions. Note that empty transitions may give rise to cycling as they do not require input characters. As an example consider the non-deterministic automaton defined by the following facts:

```
initial( q0).
final( q2).
trans( q0, b, q0).
trans( q0, a, q1).
trans( q1, a, q0).
trans( q1, b, q1).
trans( q1, b, q2).
trans( q2, q0).
```

The automaton is illustrated in Figure 7.2:

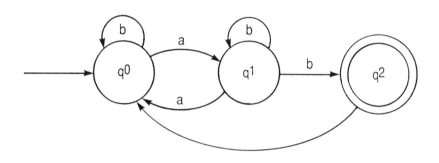

Figure 7.2 A non-deterministic automaton with an empty move, represented by the arc that has no label.

For this specific automaton the simulator should enable the following dialogue:

```
?- accept( [ a, b, b, a, b]).
yes
?- accept( [ a, b, a, a, b]).
no
```

6.

a) (*) Consider a linear arithmetic expression containing numbers (constants), one unknown denoted by 'x', and operators ' + ' and ' − '. The operator '*' is defined only for multiplying 'x' with a number (a coefficient), for example '5*x', '−17*x', ... Define the procedure 'sum(Expression, C, N)' where C is the sum of coefficients at the unknown and N is the sum of numbers, for example:

```
?- sum( 17 * x - 3 - 5 * x + 7 - 3 * x, C, N).
C = 9
N = 4
yes
```

(b) Allow the linear arithmetic expressions in (a) to also contain brackets, and extend the operator '*' to play the role of the multiplication operator on linear expressions (not allowing terms with power of 'x' higher than 1 to occur), for example '2 * x * (3 + 4 * x)' is not allowed, while '2 * x * (3 + 4)' and '2 * (3 + 4 * x)' are. Define the procedure 'sum(Expression, C, N)' that will sum up coefficients at the unknown and the numbers of such expressions.

(c) Define the procedure 'solve(Expr1 = Expr2, X)' for solving linear equations with one unknown allowing arithmetic expressions defined in (b), for example:

```
?- solve( 17*x + (20 - 3*x) - x*(25 - 100) = 12*x - (15 - 14*x) * 8, X).
X = 4
yes
```

7. (**) Partial recursive functions represent the class of computable problems, i.e. anything that is computable may be described by some partial recursive function. The latter can be constructed using the following rules:
(1) a) null function: $N(X) = 0$
   b) successor function: $S(X) = X + 1$
   c) projection function: $Uin(X1, ..., Xn) = Xi, n >= 1, 1 <= i <=$

(2) Substitution:
   If $g(X1, ..., Xn), h1(Y1, ..., Ym), ..., hn(Y1, ..., Ym)$
   are partial recursive functions, then
      $f(Y1, ..., Ym) = g(h1(Y1, ..., Ym), ..., hn(Y1, ...,Ym))$
   is also a partial recursive function.
(3) Primitive recursion:
   If $h(X1, ..., Xn)$ and $g(X1, ..., Xn, Y, Z)$ are partial
   recursive functions then the function 'f' defined by:
      $f(0, X1, ..., Xn) = h(X1, ..., Xn)$
      $f(Y+1, X1, ..., Xn) = g(X1, ..., Xn, Y, f(Y, X1, ..., Xn))$
   is also a partial recursive function.
(4) Minimization:
   If $g(X1, ..., Xn, Y)$ is a partial recursive function then the function:
      $min(Y, g(X1,..., Xn, Y)) =$ the smallest natural number Y
                                     such that $g(X1, ..., Xn, Y) = 0$
                                     if such Y exists, and undefined
                                     otherwise.
   is also a partial recursive function.

Prove that Prolog can compute anything that is computable by defining the procedure 'compute(Function, Value)' which will compute Value of Function at given values of arguments, from a given collection of functions defined by a set of facts in the form 'def(Left_hand_side = Right_hand_side)'. For example:

```
def( sum( 0, Y) = Y).              % recursive definition
def( sum( N+1, Y) = sum( N, Y+1)). % of sum
def( product( 0, Y) = 0).          % product
def( product( N+1, Y) = sum( Y, product( N, Y))).
def( difference( N, 0) = N).
def( difference( 0, Y) = 0).       % non-neg. difference
def( difference( N+1, Y) = difference( N, dec( Y))).
def( dec( 0) = 0).                 % non-negative decrement
def( dec( Y+1) = Y).
```

An example dialogue for finding the minimal natural number whose square is greater than 20 is:

```
?- compute( min( Y, difference( 20, product( Y, Y))), X).
X = 5
Y = 5
yes
```

7.3 Symbolic Logic and Logical Games

Since Prolog is based on logic, it is directly applicable to logical problems. When searching for an answer the interpreter performs logical reasoning on the facts and rules of a program. For example, assuming the procedure for the relation 'brother_or_sister' and family relations 'child' and 'parent' defined in section 1.2, we can ask Prolog who is a child of Peter's parent that is not his brother or sister:

```
?- parent( X, peter), child( X, Child),
   not( brother_or_sister( Child, peter)).
X = ann
Child = peter
yes
```

Often we can solve a logical problem in Prolog simply by stating it in a similar way as above.

Solutions to many logical problems and logical games may be easily found by using recursive programming techniques. For example, optimal playing of logical games may be achieved by the following strategy: in order to win one has to make moves that will prevent the opponent from winning.

As an example, consider the game of Nim which is played as follows. In the beginning there is an arbitrary number of piles of matches, each containing an arbitrary number of matches. On his turn, each player takes one or more matches from one pile. The winner is the one that takes the last match(es). One of the possible starting positions is given in Figure 7.3.

Figure 7.3   A starting position for Nim with four piles containing 1, 3, 5 and 5 matches, respectively.

The simple program for finding an optimal draw at each step of the game is 'win(State, Draw, Newstate)'. 'State' is a list of piles, represented by the number of matches', 'Draw' is the number of matches taken in the current draw and 'Newstate' is the state after the draw. The idea is to choose a draw so that the opponent can not win from the Newstate:

```
win( [X], X, []).              % To win take all the matches
                               % from the last pile.
win( List, X, List1) :-
   draw( List, X, List1),      % A backtrack point for
   not( win( List1, _, _)).    % choosing different draws.

draw( S, X, S1) :-             % First try taking all matches
   delete( X, S, S1).          % from one pile.
draw( S, X, S2) :-
   delete( Y, S, S1),          % see section 5.2
   between( X, 0, Y),          % see section 5.1, exercise 2 (d)
   Y1 is Y-X,
   insert( Y1, S1, S2).        % see section 5.2
```

The winning strategy of the 'draw' procedure is the following. First try to win by taking all the matches from one pile. If this does not prevent the opponent from winning, try choosing a certain number of matches from one of the piles. The first draw that would prevent the opponent from winning is the winning draw. Different draws are chosen through backtracking. There are two backtrack points: 'delete' for selecting a pile and 'between' for choosing the number of matches.

Exercises

8. (*) Define a program and state the appropriate questions for solving the following problem. Mr. Blue, Mr. Green and Mr. Brown are sitting in a park. One of them suddenly exclaims, "Our names correspond to the colours of our eyes – we have blue, green and brown eyes." "Yes," says the one with brown eyes, "but only one has the same name as the colour of his eyes." "You are right," says Mr. Blue. Does Mr. Green have green eyes?

9. Consider logical expressions constructed from variables and logical operators ' ˜ ' (negation), '&' (conjunction), 'v' (disjunction), ' = > ' (implication) and '< = >' (equivalence), given in the decreasing order of the strength with which they bind their arguments. Define the procedure 'satisfy(Expression)' which will instantiate the variables to 'true' or 'false', so that the value of Expression will be true (if that is possible). For example:

```
?- satisfy( X & Y <=> ˜ Z).
X = true
Y = true
Z = false;
X = false
Y = false
Z = true;
no
```

10. (*) Suppose we have logical expressions from propositional logic including constants and operators ' ˜ ' (negation), '&' (conjunction), 'v' (disjunction), ' = > ' (implication) and '< = > ' (equivalence), given in a decreasing order of the strength with which they bind their arguments. Here is an example of such an expression:

~ b & a & (a & ~ b => c) & (c <=> d)

Define a procedure 'transform(Expression, CNF) which will transform such an expression into an equivalent expression in conjunctive normal form (CNF). An expression in CNF is a conjunction of disjunctions of literals, for example:

pl v p2 v ~ p3) & (q1 v q2) & r1 & (~ s1 v ~ s2 v s3)

Below are the transformation rules:
1) X <=> Y --> (X => Y) & (Y => X)
2) X => Y --> ~ X v Y
3) ~ (X & Y) --> ~ X v ~ Y
4) ~ (X v Y) --> ~ X & ~ Y
5) X v Y & Z --> (X v Y) & (X v Z)
6) X & Y v Z --> (X v Z) & (Y v Z)
7) ~ (~ X) --> X

According to these rules, the above example expression is transformed to:

~ b & a & (~ a v b v c) & (~ c v d) & (~ d v c)

1. (**) The S-P problem is defined as follows. There are two numbers M and N such that < M < N < 100. Mr. S knows the sum of the two numbers and Mr. P knows their product. They both know that S knows the sum and that P knows the product. Here is their dialogue:
1) P: I don't know the numbers.
2) S: I knew that you didn't know the numbers. I don't know them either.
3) P: Now I know the numbers.
4) S: Now I know them too.

Define the procedure 'sp(M, N)' that will return the two numbers.

7.4 Parsing

In Prolog it is easy to parse expressions generated by *context free grammar* rules of the form:

non-terminal --> sequence of terminals and non-terminals

A simple context free grammar for generating the sentences 'John likes Jane' and 'John loves Jane' is the following:

sentence --> [John], verb_phrase
verb_phrase --> [likes], [Jane] | [loves], [Jane]

where square brackets denote a terminal and the symbol '|' denotes an alternative. We can define a simple parser for the above grammar:

```
sentence1( S) :-
   conc( ['John'], V, S),
   verb_phrase( V).

verb_phrase( V) :-
   conc( [likes], ['Jane'], V);
   conc( [loves], ['Jane'], V).
```

Names are written between quotes since we want them to start with uppercase initials. The input sentence is given as a list of words. The above parser allows the following dialogue:

```
?- sentence1( [ 'John', likes, 'Jane']).
yes
?- sentence1( [ 'John', hates, 'Jane']).
no
```

To speed up the execution we first define the procedure 'c' for concatenating two lists by a single fact:

```
c( [X], S, [ X| S]).
```

Using this procedure, we can rewrite the above parser by introducing an additional argument 'Rem', which indicates the remainder of the sentence not parsed by the current clause:

```
sentence2( S, Rem) :-
   c( ['John'], Rem1, S),
   verb_phrase( Rem1, Rem).

verb_phrase( V, Rem) :-
   c( [likes], Rem1, V);
   c( ['Jane'], Rem, Rem1).

verb_phrase( V, Rem) :-
   c( [loves], Rem1, V),
   c( ['Jane'], Rem, Rem1).
```

Prolog allows a special *definite clause grammar* notation for writing parsers. In this notation, the above parser is written as follows:

```
sentence3 --> ['John'], verb_phrase.
verb_phrase --> [likes], ['Jane'].
verb_phrase --> [loves], ['Jane'].
```

Prolog itself translates clauses from this notation to standard Prolog clauses by adding two arguments: the input phrase and the remainder. The procedure 'sentence3' is therefore equivalent to the procedure 'sentence2'. When parsing, two arguments are needed:

```
?- sentence3( ['John', loves, 'Jane'], []).
yes
```

By the empty list in the second argument (the remainder) we indicate that we want the whole input phrase to be parsed.

142

To show how simple it is to write a more powerful parser, let us extend the given grammar:

sentence --> noun__phrase, verb__phrase
noun__phrase --> proper__name | determiner, noun
proper__name --> ['John'] | ['Jane']
determiner --> [a] | [the]
noun --> [man] | [woman] | [programmer]
verb__phrase --> verb, noun__phrase
verb --> [likes] | [loves]

The parser for this grammar written in the definite clause grammar notation is the following:

```
sentence --> noun_phrase, verb_phrase.
noun_phrase --> proper_name.
noun_phrase --> determiner, noun.
proper_name --> ['John']; ['Jane'].
determiner --> [a]; [the].
noun --> [man]; [woman]; [programmer].
verb_phrase --> verb, noun_phrase.
verb --> [likes]; [loves].
```

Definite clause grammars are an extension of context free grammars, as they allow the introduction of arguments for storing the results of parsing. These arguments are additional to the two standard arguments – the input phrase and the remainder. Besides extra conditions in the form of Prolog procedure calls are allowed at the right-hand sides of grammar rules. These conditions must be enclosed in brackets ' { ',' } '. The disjunction operator and the cut may be used as well. To illustrate these notions, we define a parser of arithmetic expressions that sums up integers and returns the sum:

```
sum (Value) --> number( Value).
sum (Value) --> number( Value1), [+], sum (Value2),
                { Value is Value1 + Value2}.
number (N) --> [N], { integer (N)}.
```

The following dialogue is now possible:

```
?- sum( S, [ 1, '+', 2 '+', 3, '+', 4], []).
S = 10
yes
?- sum( S, [ 1, '+', 2, '+', b], []).
no
```

Note
Parsers written in the definite clause grammar notation can also be used in the opposite direction as generators of phrases. For example:

```
?- sentence3( S, []).
S = [ 'John', likes, 'Jane'];
S = [ 'John', loves, 'Jane'];
no
```

Exercises

12. Define a parser of Roman numerals that will also return the corresponding Arabic numerals, e.g.

```
?- roman( Arabic, "MDCCCXIV", []).
Arabic = 1814
yes
```

13. Define a parser of numbers from 1 to 99 written in German that will also return the corresponding Arabic numerals. For example:

```
?- german( N, [acht, und, fuenfzig], []).
N = 58
yes
```

14. (**) Suppose we have the following grammar for generating a small subset of English:

sentence --> [if], sentence, [then], sentence
sentence --> [neither], sentence, [nor], sentence
sentence --> simple_sentence, [if], sentence
sentence --> simple_sentence, [and], sentence
sentence --> simple_sentence, [or], sentence
sentence --> simple_sentence, [if], [and], [only], [if], sentence
sentence --> simple_sentence, [only], [when], sentence
sentence --> simple_sentence

simple_sentence --> noun_phrase, verb_phrase

noun_phrase --> determiner, noun, rel_clause
noun_phrase --> proper_name | quant_pronoun

verb_phrase --> trans_verb, noun_phrase
verb_phrase --> trans_verb, quant_pronoun
verb_phrase --> intrans_verb,

rel_clause --> [that], verb_phrase
rel_clause --> []   % [ ] denotes an empty word
determiner --> [every] | [a]

noun --> [man] | [woman] | [programmer] | [computer] | [school]
proper_name --> [john] | [jane] | [jordan] | [bitola] | [ljubljana]
trans_verb --> [loves] | [likes] | [hates] | [has] | [is] | [makes] | [needs] | [sees]
intrans_verb --> [lives] | [enjoys]

quant_pronoun --> neg_pronoun | univ_pronoun | indef_pronoun

neg_pronoun --> [nobody] | [nothing]
univ_pronoun --> [everybody] | [everything]
indef_pronoun --> [somebody] | [something]

Define a parser for the above grammar that will return also first order predicate logic expressions that correspond to the sentences, for example:

```
?- sentence( L, [ if, john, is, a man, and every, man, loves,
    a, woman, then, john, loves, a, woman], []).
L = exists( A, ( is( john, A), man( A))) &
    all( C, man( C) => exists( B, ( loves( C, B), woman( B))))
    => exists( D, ( loves( john, D) & woman( D)))
yes


?- sentence( L, [every, woman, that, likes, a, programmer,
    hates, a, computer], []).
L = all( A, woman( A) & exists( B, likes( A, B),
    programmer( B)) =>
    exists( C, hates( A, C), computer( C)))
yes
```

(Hint: additional arguments are needed to transfer data between noun_phrases and verb_phrases, determiner, noun and rel_clauses).

7.5. Interpreter Writing

Prolog can be used for developing compilers and interpreters, as it enables efficient manipulation of symbols. A simple interpreter of Prolog, written in Prolog itself, consists of the following four clauses:

```
execute( true).
execute(( Goal, Goals)) :-
    execute( Goal),
    execute( Goals).
execute(( Goal; Goals)) :-
    execute( Goal);
    execute( Goals).
execute( Goal) :-
    clause( Goal, Goals),       % built-in procedure
    execute( Goals).
```

The built-in procedure 'clause(Head, Body)' returns the head and the body of a program clause. In the case of a fact, the second argument is instantiated to true.

To show how Prolog can be used for developing interpreters of procedural languages, a simple interpreter of a Pascal-like language is proposed. Let the language allow only numerical variables and operations for reading, writing and arithmetic. For convenience, only lower-case letters are allowed. We will assume that a syntactically correct program is input to the interpreter as a Prolog question. Here is an example dialogue:

```
?- program test;
   var a, b, c
   begin
     read(a); read( b);
     c := sqrt( a * a + b * b);
     write( 'The length of the hypotenuse is ');
     write( c)
   end.
Type in the value of a: 3.
Type in the value of b: 4.
The length of the hypotenuse is 5.0
```

The numbers 3 and 4 were typed in by the user. The whole program was input as a single
Prolog term, therefore we have to appropriately define the following operators:

```
:- op( 200, fx, program).
:- op( 1099, fx, var).
:- op( 1150, xfx, .begin).
:- op( 800, xfx, := ).
:- op( 1140, xf, end).
```

Following the top-down approach to interpreter development, we first identify the sub-
problems: the interpreter has to accept the whole program, initialize values of variables and
interpret statements:

```
program Name; var Variables begin Statements end :-
   initialize( Variables),
   interpret( Statements).
```

We further develop the procedures for solving each sub-problem. Values of variables will be
stored as facts by using the built-in procedure 'assert/1'. Initially variables have arbitrary
values:

```
initialize(( X, Variables)) :- !,       % if there is more
   initialize( X),                       % than one variable
   initialize( Variables).
initialize( X) :-                        % Initialize to
   assert( value( X, _)).                % an arbitrary value.
```

During the interpretation, values of variables will be accessed directly with the procedure call
'value(Variable, Value)' and changed with the procedure 'change/2':

```
change( Variable, New_value) :-
   retract( value( Variable, _)),
   assert( value( Variable, New_value)).
```

The interpreter will interpret each statement separately:

```
interpret( ( S; Statements)) :- !,
   interpret( S),
   interpret( Statements).
```

The three types of statements (read, write and the assignment statement) are interpreted by separate clauses. Reading the value of a variable will change its current value:

```
interpret( read( Var)) :-
   write( 'Type in the value of '),
   write( Var),
   read( Value),
   change( Var, Value).
```

The argument of the write statement may be a variable name or an atom in the form of a string of characters:

```
interpret( write( Var)) :-
   value( Var, Value), !,
   write( Value).
interpret( write( String)) :-
   write( String).
```

It is somewhat more difficult to interpret the 'assignment' statement since arithmetic expressions may also contain variables. To solve this problem, we construct an arithmetic expression that contains only numbers:

```
interpret( Var := Arith_exp) :-
   construct( Arith_exp, Evaluable),   % make it evaluable
   Value is Evaluable,
   change( Var ,Value).

construct( Structure, Evaluable) :-
   Structure =.. [ Functor| Args],
   cons_list( Args, Eval_args),        % Construct a list of
   Evaluable = .. [ Functor| Eval_args]. % evaluable arguments.
cons_list( [],[]).
cons_list( [X|T],[E |Es]):-
   construct( X,E),
   construct( T,Es)

cons_list( [], []).
cons_list( [ X| T], [ E| Es]) :-
   construct( X, E),
   construct(T, Es).
```

Exercises

15. Assume we have a simple language implementing arithmetic operations that allows the following commands:

'load(X)'	– put X at the top of the stack; increment the stack
'add'	– sum up the two elements at the top of the stack and put the result into the lower of the two positions; decrement the stack by one
'subtract'	– subtract the element at the top of the stack from the element below it and put the result into the lower of the two positions; decrement the stack by one
'multiply'	– analogous to 'add' except that the operation is multiplication and not addition

'divide'   – analogous to 'subtract' except that the operation is division and not
                subtraction

(a) Define a procedure 'translate(Arith_expr, List_of_commands)' that will translate a
given arithmetic expression containing only numbers and operators ' + ', ' − ', ' * ' and ' / ' to
a list of commands of the above defined language. For example:

```
?- translate( 1 + 3 * 5 - ( 8 + 3), L).
L = [ load( 1), load( 3), load( 5), multiply, add, load( 8),
      load( 3), sum, subtract]
yes
```

(b) Define a procedure 'interpret(List_of_commands, Result)' which will interpret a list of
commands in the above defined language and will return the result of the original arithmetic
expression, for example:

```
?- interpret( [ load(1), load(3), load(5), multiply, add], X).
X = 16
yes
```

16. (**) Extend the interpreter of Prolog in Prolog to correctly handle the operator 'cut'.
(Hint: use the built-in procedure 'assert/1' to store the necessary information.)

17. Extend the interpreter of a Pascal-like language introduced in this section to handle the
following statements:
(a) 'if Condition then (Statements1) else (Statements2)' where Condition is of the form:
    'Arith_expression Comparison_operator Arith_expression'
    (e.g. 3 * a−b >= 2 * c)
(b) 'while Condition do (Statements)' where Condition is as in (a)
(c) 'repeat(Statements) until Condition' where Condition is as in (a)

18. (**)
(a) Define the procedure 'spy(Procedure/N)' that will cause the name of Procedure with N
arguments to be displayed at every call of the Procedure, also when backtracking. (Hint: 'spy'
should add clauses to the given procedure to control information about tracing and whether
the procedure was called for the first time or when backtracking.)

(b) Extend the procedure 'spy(Procedure/N)' from (a) to output (call Procedure(
Arguments)' when the Procedure is called for the first time and 'redo Procedure(
Arguments)' when the Procedure is called again due to backtracking. Information about the
success 'exit Procedure' and failure 'fail Procedure' of the execution of the Procedure should
also be output. The nested calls, i.e. recursive calls, should be indented. For example:

```
?- spy( member/2).
yes
?- member( 2, [ 1, 2, 3]).
call member( 2, [ 1, 2, 3])
  call member( 2, [ 2, 3])
  exit member( 2, [ 2, 3])
exit member( 2, [ 1, 2, 3])
yes
```

(c) Define the procedure 'nospy(Procedure/N)' that will undo the effect of the procedure 'spy' from (b).

7.6 Expert Systems

An *expert system* is a program that contains a large amount of knowledge from some problem domain and can solve problems like a human expert. The system must be able to explain how it derived the conclusions. In expert systems, knowledge is usually stored in the *knowledge base* by a set of facts and rules that are used to infer conclusions and to explain them.

The Prolog interpreter itself can be viewed as a simple *expert system shell*, i.e. an expert system consisting of an inference mechanism and a user interface, without a domain specific knowledge-base. As is typical for expert systems, the Prolog interpreter allows knowledge to be input in the form of facts and rules and is capable of infering conclusions demanded by the user in the form of questions. A simple explanation of *how* an answer was derived from facts and rules is provided by the trace of rules that were successfully applied in the course of execution.

Let us extend the simple Prolog interpreter from section 7.5, so that it will also return the trace of an execution. The extended interpreter can be considered as a simplified expert system shell that provides both conclusions and their explanations. In addition, let us modify the syntax of rules in order to distinguish them from our interpreter, by replacing the operator ':-' with the operator 'if', ',' with 'and' and ';' with 'or'. Below are the definitions of the operators:

```
:- op( 800, xfx, if).
:- op( 760, xfy, or).
:- op( 750, xfy, and).
```

To simplify the implementation of the shell, we change the syntax of facts into the form 'Fact if true'. The main procedure of the shell is 'answer(Question, Explanation)' which infers answers to the Question and provides their Explanation in the form of a list of rules successfully applied in the course of inference. We use the difference-list notation to efficiently implement the concatenation of lists of explanations.

```
answer( Question, Explanation) :-
    exe( Question, Explanation - []).

exe( true, X-X).                         % The right-hand side of a fact
                                         % returns an empty explanation.
exe( Q1 and Qs, Expl1-X) :-
    exe( Q1, Expl1-Expl2),               % An implicit concatenation
    exe( Qs, Expl2-X).                   % of two lists of explanations.
exe(Q1 or Qs, Expl) :-
    exe( Q1, Expl);
    exe( Qs, Expl).
exe( Q, [ Q if Body| Expl]-X) :-         % The rule is added to
    Q if Body,                           % the explanation.
    exe( Body, Expl-X).
```

Expert systems usually obtain data in a dialogue with the user. This information is usually stored in the dynamic knowledge-base in the form of facts. We can simplify the dialogue by asking the user only to confirm or to deny the information offered by the system. Let us extend the shell with a clause which will retrieve the desired information from the user if no rule is applicable. In this case, the explanation includes 'useranswer', stating that the question was confirmed by the user.

```
exe( Q, [ Q if useranswer | X]-X) :-    % If the question
   not( Q if Body), !,                  % Q was confirmed
   ask( Q, yes).                        % by the user.

ask( Q, Answer) :-
   write( 'Is it true: '),
   write( Q),
   getanswer( A),
   A = Answer.

getanswer( A) :-
   repeat,
   write(' (yes/no)? '),
   read( A),
   nl,
   (A = yes; A = no), !.                 % Only answers yes and no are allowed.
```

Suppose we have a simple knowledge-base for an expert system for the 'Lonely Hearts Marriage Agency'. This knowledge-base should be able to assure the client, when he/she is not certain whether his/her partner loves him/her. The conclusion that 'Partner loves Client' can be drawn from caricatured rules about some possible appearances of love:

```
loves( X, Y) if wants_to_marry( X, Y) and no_calculations( X, Y).
loves( X, Y) if shows_attention( X, Y).

no_calculations( X, Y) if poor( Y) or not_greedy( X).

shows_attention( X, Y) if man( X) and buys( X, Y, flowers).
shows_attention( X, Y) if woman( X) and dresses_up_for(X,Y).

man( tim) if true.
man( john) if true.

woman( jane) if true.
woman( mary) if true.
```

The following dialogue is then possible:

```
?- answer( loves( tim, jane), Explanation).
Is it true: wants_to_marry( tim, jane) (yes/no)? yes.
Is it true: poor( jane) (yes/no)? no.
Is it true: not_greedy( tim) (yes/no)? no.
Is it true: buys( tim, jane, flowers) (yes/no)? yes.
Explanation = [ loves( tim, jane) if shows_attention( tim,
   jane), shows_attention( tim, jane) if man( tim) and buys(
   tim, jane, flowers), man( tim) if true, buys( tim, jane,
   flowers) if useranswer]
yes
```

Exercises

19. Extend the shell to display the explanation in a more readable form:

Goal was derived by rule:
   IF Condition1 AND Condition2
      THEN Goal

Condition1 was derived by rule:
   IF Condition3
      THEN Condition1

Condition3 was confirmed by the user

Condition2 was found as a fact

20. Change the shell so that it will not ask the same question twice and that it will ask the user only questions marked by the facts 'askable(Question)'.

21. (*) Extend the shell from exercise 20 so that it will not provide only the explanation 'how' it derived an answer, but also the explanation *why* the user's answer is needed. So, instead of only answering 'yes' or 'no' to the given questions, the user may also answer 'why', causing the system to display the sequence of inferences that are currently being performed to answer the original question. The dialogue continues by repeating the question to the user. For example:

```
?- answer( loves( tim, jane)).
Is it true: wants_to_marry( tim, jane) (yes/no/why)? yes.
Is it true: poor( jane) (yes/no/why)? why.

I am trying to prove no_calculations( tim, jane) by rule:
  IF poor( jane) OR
    not_greedy( tim)
    THEN no_calculations( tim, jane)
  because:
I am trying to prove loves( tim, jane) by rule:
  IF wants_to_marry( tim, jane) AND no_calculations( tim, jane)
    THEN loves( tim, jane)
  because:
 this was your original question

Is it true: poor( jane) (yes/no/why)? no.
Is it true: not_greedy( tim) (yes/no/why)? no.
Is it true: buys( tim, jane, flowers) (yes/no/why)? yes.

The answer is yes, here is the explanation:

loves( tim, jane) was derived by rule:
  IF shows_attention( tim, jane)
    THEN loves( tim, jane)
```

```
shows_attention( tim, jane) was derived by rule:
  IF man( tim) AND buys( tim, jane, flowers)
    THEN shows_attention( tim, jane)


man( tim) was found as a fact


buys( tim, jane, flowers) was confirmed by the user


yes
```

22. (**) Extend the shell from exercise 21 with a simple *probabilistic mechanism* which handles facts and rules that are believed to be true only to a certain extent, determined with a *certainty factor* C, a number between 0 and 1. In this scheme, rules and facts have the form:

Conclusion with C if Condition.

The certainty factor of a Conclusion is a product of C and the certainty factor of a Condition. If Condition is believed to be true with certainty C1 then the Conclusion is believed to be true with certainty $C*C1$. In case of a conjunctive Condition where:

Condition = Condition1 and Condition2 and ... and ConditionN

the certainty factor C of a Condition is obtained as a minimum, i.e. $C = min(Ci)$ for i $= 1$, ... , n. In case of a disjunctive Condition where

Condition = Condition1 or Condition2 or ... or ConditionN

the certainty factor C is obtained as a maximun, i.e. $C = max(Ci)$ for i $= 1$, ..., n.

When programming this extension of the shell note that:
− the execution will now always succeed and the answer will contain the certainty factor expressing the degree of belief that the answer to the original question is 'yes',
−'a if b. a if c.' is equivalent to 'a if b or c' (when trying to prove a given goal, all rules for that goal should be considered in order to find the rule that confirms the goal with the greatest certainty factor),
− the explanation of answers should contain only rules which return the maximal certainty factor for the goal in question,
− when answering 'why', it is not necessary to display the certainty factor, while when displaying 'how' explanations it is.

For example:

```
?- answer( loves( tim, jane)).
How sure are you that wants_to_marry( tim, jane) is true
(0..1/why)? 0.9.
How sure are you that poor( jane) is true (0..1/why)? 0.1.
How sure are you that not_greedy( tim) is true (0..1/why)? 0.2.
How sure are you that buys( tim, jane, flowers) is true
(0..1/why)? 0.9.

The answer is yes with certainty: 0.729 Here is the explanation:

loves( tim, jane) was derived with certainty 0.729 by rule:
  IF shows_attention( tim, jane)
    THEN loves( tim, jane) with certainty 0.9

shows_attention( tim, jane) was derived with certainty 0.81 by rule:
  IF man( tim) AND buys( tim, jane, flowers)
    THEN shows_attention( tim, jane) with certainty 0.9

man( tim) was found as a fact with certainty 1.0

buys( tim, jane, flowers) was confirmed by the user with certainty 0.9

yes
```

7.8 Solutions to Exercises

1.
```
transform( Tree, List) :-
  trans_list( Tree, List, []).

% The third argument of 'trans_list' is the part of a list that
% remains after the left sublist corresponding to the left
% subtree is considered.

trans_list( nil, [ nil| Tail], Tail).
trans_list( btree( X, Left, Right), [ X| Tail], Rest):-
  trans_list( Left, Tail, Rest1),
  trans_list( Right, Rest1, Rest).
```

2. (a)
```
in( X, dict( X, _, _)) :- !.
in( X, dict( Y, Left, Right)) :-
  X < Y, !,
  in( X, Left).
in( X, dict( Y, Left, Right)) :-
  X > Y,
  in( X, Right).
```

(b)
```
add( X, nil, dict( X, nil, nil)).        % add to the empty subtree
add( X, dict( X, Left, Right), dict( X, Left, Right)) :- !.
add( X, dict( Y, Left, Right), dict( Y, Left, Newright)) :-
   X > Y, !,
   add( X, Right, Newright).
add( X, dict( Y, Left, Right), dict( Y, Newleft, Right)) :-
   X < Y,
   add( X, Left, Newleft).
```

(c)
```
del( X, nil, nil) :- !.
del( X, dict( Y, Left, Right), dict( Y, Left, Newright)) :-
   X > Y, !,
   del( X, Right, Newright).
del( X, dict( Y, Left, Right), dict( Y, Newleft, Right)) :-
   X < Y, !,
   del( X, Left, Newleft).
del( X, dict( X, nil, Right), Right) :- !.
del( X, dict( X, Left, nil), Left) :- !.
   % If one of the subtrees is empty, the new tree is the
   % remaining subtree, otherwise the rightmost number from
   % the left subtree is the root of the tree.
del( X, dict( X, Left, Right), dict( N, Newleft, Right)) :-
   right_most( Left, N, Newleft).


right_most( dict( X, Left, nil), X, Left) :- !.
right_most( dict( X, Left, Right), N, dict( X, Left, Newright)) :-
   right_most( Right, N, Newright).
```

3.
```
min_path( X, Y, Path) :-
   find_path( Y, [[ X]], Path).
% The second argument is a list of paths that were already
% examined. They are candidates for the solution path. At each
% step, an element of this candidate set is examined and all
% possible one-step extensions are added at the end of the list.


find_path( Y, List, Path) :-
   member( [ X| Tail], List),        % see section 5.2
   arc( X, Y), !,
   reverse( [ Y, X| Tail], Path).    % exercise 10 in section 5.2
% In this case a candidate set contains a path that will reach
% the goal after its one-step extension.
```

```
find_path( Y, List, Path) :-
  setof(
    [ Z, X| Tail],
    (member( [ X| Tail], List),
     arc( X, Z),
     not( member( Z, [ X| Tail]))),   % to prevent cyclic paths
    NewList),
  find_path( Y, NewList, Path).
% 'setof' generates all one-step extensions of candidate paths.
```

4. The following clauses have to be added at the top of the procedure 'd' for symbolic derivation from section 7.2:

```
d( U^C, X, 0) :- C =:= 0, !.
d( U^C, X, C  U^C1 * DU) :- !,
  C =\= 0,
  C1 is C - 1,
  d( U, X, DU).
d( exp( U), X, exp( U) * DU) :- !, d( U, X, DU).
d( sin( U), X, cos( U) * DU) :- !, d( U, X, DU).
d( cos( U), X, - sin( U) * DU) :- !, d( U, X, DU).
d( tan( U), X, 1 / ( cos( U)^2) * DU) :- !, d( U, X, DU).
d( ln( U), X, 1 / U * DU) :- !, d( U, X, DU).
```

5. Non-determinism is an inherent property of execution of Prolog programs, therefore the only additional thing to be considered is preventing cycling due to empty transactions.

```
accept( Word) :-
  initial( State),
  accept( State, Word).


accept( State, []) :-
  empty( State, State1),
  final( State1).
accept( State, [ X| Word]) :-
  empty( State, State1),
  trans( State1, X, State2),
  accept( State2, Word).


% Make an arbitrary number of empty transactions without cycling.
% When cycling occurs, the procedure 'empty( S, S1, Trace)' fails.

empty( S, S1) :- empty( S, S1, [S]).   % the third argument is the trace


empty( S, S, _).
empty( S, S1, Trace) :-
  trans( S, S2),
  not( member( S2, Trace)),            % see section 5.2.
  empty( S2, S1, [ S2| Trace]).
```

155

6. (a)

```
sum( X + Y, C, N) :- !,
  term( Y, C1, N1),
  sum( X, C2, N2),                    % recursive definition
  C is C1 + C2,
  N is N1 + N2.
sum( X - Y, C, N) :- !,
  term( Y, C1, N1),
  sum( X, C2, N2),
  C is C2 - C1,
  N is N2 - N1.
sum(  -  X, C, N) :- !,
  term( X, C1, N1),
  C is - C1,
  N is - N1.
sum( X, C, N) :- term( X, C, N).

term( x, 1, 0) :- !.
term( C * x, C, 0) :- number( C), !.
term( N, 0, N) :- number( N), !.
```

(b) The procedure 'sum(Expr, C, N)' is the same as in (a), only the procedure 'term(Term, C, N)' is changed to:

```
term( X * Y, C, N) :- !,
  factor( X, CX, NX),
  term( Y, CY, NY),
  C is CX * NY + NX * CY,              % note that the coefficient
  N is NX * NY.                        % CX * CY at 'x' square is
                                       % ignored.
term( X, C, N) :-
  factor( X, C, N).

% when using brackets, factor may be a sum of terms or one term,
% otherwise it is a number or the unknown 'x'

factor( X + Y, C, N) :- !,
  sum( X + Y, C, N).
factor( X - Y, C, N) :- !,
  sum( X - Y, C, N).
factor( -X, C, N) :- !,
  sum( -X, C, N).
factor( X * Y, C, N) :- !,
  term( X * Y, C, N).
factor( N, 0, N) :- number( N), !.
factor( x, 1, 0).
```

(c)
```
solve( Left = Right, X) :-
  sum( Left, CL, NL),
  sum( Right, CR, NR),
  C is CL - CR,
  N is NR - NL,
  C =\= 0,
  X is N / C.
```

7.
```prolog
compute( 0, 0) :- !.                    % null function
compute( X + 1, X1) :- !, X1 is X + 1.  % successor
compute( X, X) :- number( X), !.        % projection
compute( min( Y, G), Y) :- !,           % minimization
   find_min( Y, G).
compute( Fun, Value) :- !,
   Fun =.. [ F| Args],
   compute_list( Args, Arg1),           % compute arguments
   Cfun =.. [ F| Arg1], !,
   def( Fun1 = Fun2),                   % find appropriate definition
   correspond( Cfun, Fun1), !,
   compute( Fun2, Value).               % compute the right-hand side
                                        % of a definition

% compute values of elements of a list:

compute_list( [], []).
compute_list( [ X| Arg], [ C| Const]) :-
   compute( X, C), !,
   compute_list( Arg, Const).

% functions correspond if they match or/except when they
% differ in the first argument, where the first argument
% of the second function is in the form Y + 1 (primitive
% recursion)

correspond( F, F) :- !.
correspond( F1, F) :-
   F =.. [ G, Y+1| Arg],
   F1 =.. [ G, N| Arg], !,
   Y is N - 1.

% minimization: find minimal Y for which G = 0

find_min( Y, G) :-
   give( Y),                            % generate natural numbers
   compute( G, 0).

give( 0).
give( Y1) :-
   give( Y),
   Y1 is Y + 1.
```

8.
```prolog
names( [ green, blue, brown]).          % all the names

% find all possible mappings between names and eye colours
% respecting the given restrictions:
% 1. Mr. Blue can not have brown eyes.
% 2. Exactly one has the name that corresponds to his eye
%    colour.
%
% A mapping has the form :
% [ name1/colour1, name2/colour2, name3/colour3]
%
```

```
possible_colours( List) :-
  names( Names),
  names( Colours),
  findall( Names_colours,                % see exercise 16 in section 5.3.
         ( permut( Colours, Pcolours),
           map( Names, Pcolours, Names_colours),
         % map names to colours
           not( member( blue/brown, Names_colours)),
         % Mr. Blue can not have brown eyes
           member( X/X, Names_colours),
         % one must have the same name and eye colour
           not(( member( Y/Y, Names_colours),
           Y \== X))),
         % but nobody else may have the same name and eye colour
         List).


% map the list of names and the list of colours into one list:

map( [], [], []).
map([ Name| Names], [ Colour| Colours], [ Name/Colour| Ns_Cs]) :-
  map( Names, Colours, Ns_Cs).


% return all permutations of the list through backtracking:

permut( [], []).
permut( [ X| Tail], Perm) :-
  permut( Tail, Perm1),
  insert( X, Perm1, Perm).                % see section 5.2.

% The question that solves the problem is:
%
% is there a possible mapping Ns_Cs of colours from List of
% all possible mappings which says that Mr. Green has green
% eyes?

?- possible_colours( List), member( Ns_Cs, List),
   member( green/green, Ns_Cs).

% (the answer is 'no')


9.
  :- op( 200, fy, ~).
  :- op( 300, xfy, & ).
  :- op( 400, xfy, v ).
  :- op( 500, xfx, => ).
  :- op( 600, xfx, <=> ).

  satisfy( true) :- !.
  satisfy( X & Y) :- satisfy( X), satisfy( Y).
  satisfy( X v Y) :- satisfy( X); satisfy( Y).
  satisfy( X => Y) :- satisfy( Y v ~ X).
  satisfy( X <=> Y) :- satisfy(( Y => X) & ( X => Y)).
  satisfy( ~ X) :- not_satisfy( X).
```

```
not_satisfy( false) :- !.
not_satisfy( X & Y) :- not_satisfy( X); not_satisfy( Y).
not_satisfy( X v Y) :- not_satisfy( X), not_satisfy( Y).
not_satisfy( X => Y) :- not_satisfy( Y v ~ X). '
not_satisfy( X <=> Y) :- not_satisfy( ( Y => X) & ( X => Y)).
not_satisfy( ~ X) :- satisfy( X).
```

10.
```
:- op( 100, fy, ~ ).
:- op( 110, xfy, &).
:- op( 120, xfy, v).
:- op( 130, xfx, =>).
:- op( 140, xfx, <=>).
:- op( 160, fx, if).
:- op( 170, xfx, else).
:- op( 180, xfx, then).


transform( T1, T2) :-
  trans( T1, T-[]),            % use the difference-list notation
  change_list( T, T2).        % change a list to a conjunction


trans( S1 & S2, T1-D) :- !,
  trans( S1, T1-T2),
  trans( S2, T2-D).
trans( S, T) :-
  if ( one( S, S1), !)         % see exercise 7 in section 6.2
    then trans( S1, T)
    else ( [S|X]-X = T).       % T is a list of conjuncts


% make one transformation if possible, otherwise fail:


one( X <=> Y, (X => Y) & (Y => X)).
one( X => Y, ~ X v Y).
one( ~ (X v Y), ~ X & ~ Y).
one( ~ (X & Y), ~ X v ~ Y).
one( X v Y & Z, (X v Y) & (X v Z)).
one( X & Y v Z, (X v Z) & (Y v Z)).
one( ~ (~ X), X).
one( X v Y, X v Y1) :-
  one( Y, Y1).
one( X v Y, X1 v Y) :-
  one( X, X1).
one( ~ X, ~ X1) :-
  one( X, X1).


% make a conjunction of elements of a given list:


change_list( [X], X) :- !.
change_list( [ X, Y| Tail], X & T) :-
  change_list( [ Y| Tail], T).
```

159

11.

```prolog
sp( M, N) :-
  between( S, 4, 198),              % S is between 4 and 198
                                    % see exercise 2 (d) in section 5.1
  conclusion4( S, P),               % find P
  S2 is (S div 2) + 1,
  between( M, 1, S2),               % find corresponding M and N
  N is S-M,
  P is M * N.

% conclusion1: a product P corresponds to several (i.e. at least
% two) sum values S:

conclusion1( P) :- setof( S, correspond( S, P), [_,_|_]), !.

% conclusion2: for every P that corresponds to S the
%               conclusion1( P) is true and there are several P-s
%               that correspond to S:

conclusion2( S) :-
  setof( P, correspond( S, P), [ P1, P2| Ps]), !,
  check( [ P1, P2| Ps]), !.

% for all the elements of the list the conclusion1 is true:

check( []).
check([ P| Ps]) :-
  conclusion1( P),
  check( Ps).

% conclusion3: there is exactly one S that corresponds to P
%               for which the conclusion2 is true:

conclusion3( P, S) :-
  setof( S1, (correspond( S1, P), conclusion2( S1)), [ S]), !.

% conclusion4: there is exactly one P that correspond to S
%               for which the conclusion3 is true:

conclusion4( S, P1) :-
  setof( P, ( correspond( S, P), conclusion3( P, S)), [ P1]), !.
% sum S and product P correspond:
correspond( S, P) :-
  integer( S),                      % if S is known
  S1 is (S div 2) + 1,
  between( M, 1, S1),               % backtrack point
  P is M * (S - M).
correspond( S, P) :-
  integer( P),                      % if P is known
  P1 is P div 2,
  between( M, 1, P1),               % backtrack point
  N is P div M,
  N > M,
  P is M * N,
  S is M + N.
```

160

12.
```
roman(4) --> roman1( 1), roman1( 5), !.
roman(9) --> roman1( 1), roman1( 10), !.
roman(A) --> roman1( A1), roman( A2), { A is A1 + A2}.
roman(A) --> roman1( A).


roman1(1) --> "I".
roman1(5) --> "V".
roman1(10) --> "X".
roman1(50) --> "L".
roman1(100) --> "C".
roman1(500) --> "D".
roman1(1000) --> "M".
```

13.
```
german(N) --> digit( N).
german(N) --> teen( N).
german(N) --> tens( N).
german(N) --> digit( D), [und], tens( T), { N is T + D}.


digit(1) --> [ein].
digit(2) --> [zwei].
digit(3) --> [drei].
digit(4) --> [vier].
digit(5) --> [fuenf].
digit(6) --> [sechs].
digit(7) --> [sieben].
digit(8) --> [acht].
digit(9) --> [neun].

teen(10) --> [zehn].
teen(11) --> [elf].
teen(12) --> [zwoelf].
teen(13) --> [dreizehn].
teen(14) --> [vierzehn].
teen(15) --> [fuenfzehn].
teen(16) --> [sechzehn].
teen(17)  -> [siebzehn].
teen(18)  -> [achtzehn].
teen(19) --> [neunzehn].


tens(20) --> [zwanzig].
tens(30) --> [dreissig].
tens(40) --> [vierzig].
tens(50) --> [fuenfzig].
tens(60) --> [sechzig].
tens(70) --> [siebzig].
tens(80) --> [achtzig].
tens(90) --> [neunzig].
```

161

14.

```
:- op( 150, fy, neg).                % negation
:- op( 160, xfy, & ).                % conjunction
:- op( 170, xfy, v ).                % disjunction
:- op( 200, xfx, => ).               % implication
:- op( 210, xfx, <=> ).              % equivalence

sentence( P => Q) -->
  [if], sentence( P), [then], sentence( Q).
sentence( P => Q) -->
  simple_sentence( Q), [if], sentence( P).
sentence( neg P & neg Q) -->
  [neither], sentence( P), [nor], sentence( Q).
sentence( P & Q) -->
  simple_sentence( P), [and], sentence( Q).
sentence( P v Q) -->
  simple_sentence( P), [or], sentence( Q).
sentence( P <=> Q) -->
  simple_sentence( P), [if, and, only, if], sentence( Q).
sentence( P <=> Q) -->
  simple_sentence( P), [ only, when], sentence( Q).
sentence( P) --> simple_sentence( P).


simple_sentence( P) -->
  noun_phrase( X, P1, P), verb_phrase( X, P1).


% noun_phrase( Object, Verb_phrase, Sentence):


noun_phrase( X, P1, P) -->
  determiner( X, P2, P1, P),
  noun( X, P3),
  rel_clause( X, P3, P2).
noun_phrase( X, P, P) --> proper_name( X).
noun_phrase( X, P1, P) --> quant_pronoun( X, P1, P).


% verb_phrase( Object, Predicate):


verb_phrase( X, P) -->
  trans_verb( X, Y, P1), noun_phrase( Y, P1, P).
verb_phrase( X, P) -->
  trans_verb( X, Y, P1), quant_pronoun( Y, P1, P).
verb_phrase( X, P) -->
  intrans_verb( X, P).


rel_clause( X, P1, ( P1 & P2)) -->
  [that], verb_phrase( X, P2).
rel_clause( _, P, P) --> [].


% determiner( Object, Object_noun, Verb_predicate, Whole_exp):


determiner( X, P1, P2, all( X, (P1 => P2))) --> [every].
determiner( X, P1, P2, exists( X, (P1 & P2))) --> [a].
```

162

```
noun( X, man( X)) --> [man].
noun( X, woman( X)) --> [woman].
noun( X, programmer( X)) --> [programmer].
noun( X, computer( X)) --> [computer].
noun( X, school( X)) --> [school].


proper_name( jane) --> [jane].
proper_name( john) --> [john].
proper_name( jordan) --> [jordan].
proper_name( bitola) --> [bitola].
proper_name( ljubljana) --> [ljubljana].


% trans_verb( Object, Subject, Predicate):

trans_verb( X, Y, loves( X, Y)) --> [loves].
trans_verb( X, Y, likes( X, Y)) --> [likes].
trans_verb( X, Y, hates( X, Y)) --> [hates].
trans_verb( X, Y, has( X, Y)) --> [has].
trans_verb( X, Y, is( X, Y)) --> [is].
trans_verb( X, Y, makes( X, Y)) --> [makes].
trans_verb( X, Y, needs( X, Y)) --> [needs].
trans_verb( X, Y, sees( X, Y)) --> [sees].


% intrans_verb( Object, Predicate):

intrans_verb( X, lives(X)) --> [lives].
intrans_verb( X, eats(X)) --> [eats].
intrans_verb( X, enjoys(X)) --> [enjoys].


% quant_pronoun( Subject, Trans_verb_pred, Verb_phrase):

quant_pronoun( X, P, all( X, P)) --> univ_pronoun.
quant_pronoun( X, P, exists( X, P)) --> indef_pronoun.
quant_pronoun( X, P, all( X, neg P)) --> neg_pronoun.


neg_pronoun --> [nobody].
neg_pronoun --> [nothing].


univ_pronoun --> [everybody].
univ_pronoun --> [everything].


indef_pronoun --> [somebody].
indef_pronoun --> [something].
```

5.
a)
```
% the difference-list notation is used to speed up execution:

translate( A, L) :- tr( A, L-[]).
```

163

```
      tr( X + Y, L-D) :-
         tr( X, L-L1),
         tr( Y, L1-[add|D]).
      tr( X-Y, L-D) :-
         tr( X, L-L1),
         tr( Y, L1-[subtract|D]).
      tr( X * Y, L-D) :-
         tr( X, L-L1),
         tr( Y, L1-[multiply|D]).
      tr( X / Y, L-D) :-
         tr( X, L-L1),
         tr( Y, L1-[divide|D]).
      tr( X, [load(X)|D]-D) :- number(X).
```

(b)
```
   interpret( List, Solution) :-
      in( List, [], Solution).          % initialize by an empty stack

   in( [], [S], S).                     % the result is the single remaining elemen
                                        % on the stack
   in( [ load(X)| Coms], Stack, S) :-
      in( Coms, [ X| Stack], S).
   in( [ add| Coms], [ X, Y| Stack], S) :-
      Z is X + Y,
      in( Coms, [ Z| Stack], S).
   in( [ subtract| Coms], [ X, Y| Stack], S) :-
      Z is Y - X,
      in( Coms, [ Z| Stack], S).
   in( [ multiply| Coms], [ X, Y| Stack], S) :-
      Z is X * Y,
      in( Coms, [ Z| Stack], S).
   in( [ divide| Coms], [ X, Y| Stack], S) :-
      Z is Y / X,
      in( Coms, [ Z| Stack], S).
```

16.
```
   execute( true).
   execute( !).                 % first time simply succeeds
   execute( !) :-               % When backtracking fail and ensure
      !,                        % that every goal behind the cut
      not( cut),                % including the parent goal will fail
      assert( cut), !,          % by asserting a special flag 'cut' if
      fail.                     % it is not yet asserted.
   execute( ( Goal1, Goals)) :-
      execute( Goal1),
      (execute( Goals);
       cut, !, fail).           % when backtracking to Goal1:
                                % if cut then fail

   execute( (Goal1; Goals)) :-
      execute( Goal1);
      cut, !, fail;             % when backtracking to Goals:
                                % if cut then fail
      execute( Goals).
   execute( Goal) :-
      clause( Goal, Goals),
      (execute( Goals);
       cut, retract( cut), !, fail).
```

164

```
% when backtracking to the parent goal: if cut then remove the
% flag and fail
```

7. The interpreter is extended with the following clauses:

a)
```
:- op( 800, fx, if).
:- op( 799, xfx, then).
:- op( 798, xfx, else).

% if - then - else:

interpret( if Condition then S1 else S2) :- !,
    make_eval( Condition, Eval_cond), !,
    if Eval_cond then interpret( S1) % see exercise 7 in section 6.2
              else interpret( S2).

% make a condition evaluable:

make_eval( C, E) :-
    C =.. [ Op, A1, A2],
    construct( A1, E1),            % see section 7.5
    construct( A2, E2),
    E =.. [ Op, E1, E2].
```

b)
```
:- op( 800, fx, while).
:- op( 799, xfx, do).

% while - do:

interpret( while Condition do S) :- !,
    make_eval( Condition, Eval_cond), !, % see (a)
    if Eval_cond then ( interpret( S), !,
                        interpret( while Condition do S))
              else true.
```

c)
```
:- op( 800, fx, repeat).
:- op( 799, xfx, until).

% repeat - until:

interpret( repeat S until Condition) :-
    interpret( S),!,
    make_eval( Condition, Eval_cond), !, % see (a)
    if Eval_cond then true
              else interpret( repeat S until Condition).
```

18. The procedure 'spy(P/N)' adds two clauses to the procedure P that is to be traced. The first clause of the extended procedure P will call the procedure recursively, ensuring that the recursive call will skip the first two clauses of the procedure by temporarily removing a flag. The second clause will return a flag removed by the first clause and fail, to enable the execution of the original clauses of the procedure.

(a)

```
spy( Proc/N) :-
  length1( L, N),
  Head =.. [ Proc| L],            % make the head of a procedure
  assert( tracing( Proc/N)),      % flag
  % assert the second clause to the top of the procedure:
  asserta( ( Head :- assert( tracing( Proc/N)), fail)),
  % assert the first clause to the top of the procedure:
  asserta( ( Head :-
             tracing(Proc/N),               % if tracing then:
             retract( tracing( Proc/N)),     % temporarily remove
                                             % the flag
             nl, write( Proc), !,            % write the procedure name
             call( Head),                    % call the procedure recursivel
             backtrack_output( Proc)         % treat backtracking )).

% Output the procedure name only when backtracking, without
% affecting backtracking:

backtrack_output( Proc) :-
  true;                           % in forward execution succeed
  nl, write( Proc),               % when backtracking write procedure name
  !, fail.                        % and fail

% make the list of a given length:

length1( [], 0) :- !.
length1( [ _| Y], N) :-
  N > 0,
  N1 is N - 1,
  length1( Y, N1).
```

(b)

```
spy( Proc/N) :-
  length1( L, N),                 % see (a)
  Head =.. [ Proc| L],            % make the head of the procedure
  assert( tracing( Proc/N)),      % flag
  assert( level( Proc/N, 0)),     % initialize the level of a
                                  % recursive call
  % assert the second clause to the top of the procedure:
  asserta( (Head :- assert( tracing( Proc/N)), fail)),
  % assert the first clause to the top of the procedure:
  asserta((Head :-
           tracing( Proc/N),      % if tracing then:
           retract( tracing( Proc/N)),   % temporarily remove
                                         % the flag
           level( Proc/N, Level, +1),    % increment level
           tab( Level),                  % indent with Level blanks
           write( 'call '),              % the 'call' port
           write( Head), nl, !,          % write the procedure call
           (call( Head),                 % call the procedure recursivel
            tab( Level),
            write( 'exit '),             % the 'exit' port
            write( Head), nl,            % write the procedure call
```

166

```
                level( Proc/N, _, -1),        % decrement level
                % treat backtracking:
                backtrack_output( Proc/N, Level, Head);
                % when failing do the same:
                tab( Level),                  % indent
                write( 'fail '),              % the 'fail' port
                write( Head),nl,              % write the procedure call
                level( Proc/N, _, -1),        % decrement level
                !, fail                       % and fail
              )
          )).


% Output 'redo' and procedure call only when backtracking,
% without affecting backtracking:


backtrack_output( Proc, Level, Head) :-
    true;                              % in forward execution succeed
    % when failing do:
    tab( Level),                      % indent
    write( 'redo '),                  % the 'redo' port
    write( Head), nl,                 % write the procedure call
    level( Proc, _, +1),              % increment level
    !, fail.                          % and fail


% change the current level of a recursive call of the procedure
% and return the previous level:


level( Proc, Previous, S) :-
    retract( level( Proc, Previous)),
    Current is Previous + S,
    assert( level( Proc, Current)), !.
```

c)
```
  nospy( Proc/N) :-
      tracing( Proc/N),                  % if succeeds then continue
      length1( L, N),                    % see (a)
      Head =.. [ Proc| L],
      retract( tracing( Proc/N)),        % remove flag
      retract( (Head :- _ )),            % Remove first two clauses
      retract( (Head :- _ )),            % of a procedure.
      retract( level( Proc/N,_)), !.     % remove the 'level' flag
```

9.
We define the top level procedure 'answer/1':

```
  answer( Question) :-
      answer( Question, Explanation),        % see section 7.6.
      write_list( [ nl, 'The answer is yes, here is the explanation:',
                  nl, nl]),        % see exercise 20 in section 5.5
      display_expl( Explanation).
```

167

```prolog
% display explanation:

display_expl( []).
display_expl( [ Q if true| Rules]) :- !,
   write_list( [ Q,' was found as a fact', nl, nl]),
   display_expl( Rules).
display_expl( [ Q if useranswer| Rules]) :- !,
   write_list( [ Q,' was confirmed by the user', nl, nl]),
   display_expl( Rules).
display_expl( [ Q if Body| Rules]) :-
   write_list( [ Q,' was derived by rule:', nl]),
   write_rule( Q, Body), nl,
   display_expl( Rules).


write_rule( Q, B) :-
   write( ' IF '),
   write_body( B), nl,
   write_list( [ ' THEN ', Q, nl]).


write_body( Q and Qs) :- !,
   write_body( Q), write( ' AND '), write_body( Qs).
write_body( Q or Qs) :- !,
   write_body( Q), write_list([ ' OR', nl, ' ']),
   write_body( Qs).
write_body( Q) :-
   write(Q).
```

20.

We redefine the procedure 'ask' from section 7.6 as follows:

```prolog
ask( Q, Answer) :- known( Q, Answer), !.
ask( Q, Answer) :-
   askable( Q), !,
   write_list( [ 'Is it true: ', Q]),     % see exercise 20 in section 5.5
   getanswer( A),                         % see section 7.6
   asserta( known( Q, A)), !,
   A = Answer.
```

21. In order to display a sequence of inferences the system is currently trying to make, it has to mantain the chain of rules from the original question to the current goal as the third argument of the procedure 'exe':

```prolog
answer( Question, Explanation) :-
   exe( Question, Explanation-[], []).
      % The third argument is the chain of rules from the original
      % question to the current goal.
   exe( true, X-X, _) :- !.            % The right-hand side of a fact
                                       % returns an empty explanation.
   exe( Q1 and Qs, Expl1-X, Trace) :- !,
      exe( Q1, Expl1-Expl2, Trace),    % An implicit concatenation
      exe( Qs, Expl2-X, Trace).        % of two lists of explanations.
```

```
exe( Q1 or Qs, Expl, Trace) :- !,
  (exe( Q1, Expl, Trace);
   exe( Qs, Expl, Trace)).
exe( Q, [ Q if Body| Expl]-X, Trace) :-
  Q if Body,
  exe( Body, Expl-X, [ Q if Body| Trace]).
exe( Q, [ Q if useranswer| X]-X, Trace) :-   % Q was confirmed
  not( Q if Body), !,                        % by the user.
  ask( Q, A, Trace), !,
  A = yes.

ask( Q, Answer, _) :- known( Q, Answer), !.
ask( Q, Answer, Trace) :-
  askable( Q), !,
  write_list( [ 'Is it true: ', Q]),        % see exercise 20 in section 5.5
  getanswer( A),
  treat( A, Q, Answer, Trace).

getanswer( A) :-
  repeat,
    write(' (yes/no/why)? '),
    read( A),
    nl,
  (A = yes; A = no; A = why), !.

treat( yes, Q, yes, _) :- assert( known( Q, yes)), !.
treat( no, Q, no, _) :- assert( known( Q, no)), !.
treat( why, Q, Answer, Trace) :-
  nl,
  display_trace( Trace),
  ask( Q, Answer, Trace).

display_trace( []) :-
  write( 'this was your original question'), nl, nl.
display_trace( [ Q if Body| Trace]) :-
  write_list( [ 'I am trying to prove ', Q, ' by rule:', nl]),
  write_rule( Q, Body),                      % see exercise 19
  write( ' because:'), nl,
  display_trace( Trace).

2.
:- op( 800, xfx, if).
:- op( 760, xfx, with).
:- op( 750, xfy, and).
:- op( 760, xfy, or).

answer( Question) :-
  answer( Question, Explanation, Certainty),
  write_list( [nl, 'The answer is yes with certainty: ', Certainty,
               nl, ' Here is the explanation:', nl, nl]),
  display_expl( Explanation).

answer( Question, Explanation, C) :-
  exe( Question, Explanation-[], [], C).
```

```
exe( true, X-X, _, 1) :- !.                    % The right-hand side of a fact
                                               % returns an empty explanation
                                               % and the certainty 1.
exe( Q1 and Qs, Expl1-X, Trace, C) :- !,
  exe( Q1, Expl1-Expl2, Trace, C1),            % An implicit concatenation
  exe( Qs, Expl2-X, Trace, C2),                % of two lists of explanations.
  min( C1, C2, C).
exe( Q1 or Qs, Expl, Trace, C) :- !,
  exe( Q1, Expl1, Trace, C1),
  exe( Qs, Expl2, Trace, C2),
  best_one( [ (Expl1, C1), ( Expl2, C2)], Expl, C).
exe( Q, Expl, Trace, C) :-
  best( Q, Expl, Trace, C).
exe( Q, [ Q with C if useranswer| X]-X, Trace, C) :-   % Q was
  not( Q with C1 if Body), !,                  % confirmed by the user
  ask( Q, C, Trace).                           % with certainty C.

% find a clause that confirms Q with the highest certainty:

best( Q, Expl, Trace, C) :-
  findall( ( [ Q with C1 and C3 if Body | Expl1]-X, C3),
         ( Q with C1 if Body,
           exe( Body, Expl1-X, [ Q if Body| Trace], C2),
           C3 is C1 * C2),                     % the resulting certainty
         [ S1| Set]),                          % we must get a non-empty set
  best_one( [ S1| Set], Expl, C).              % choose the highest
                                               % certainty with the
                                               % corresponding explanation

best_one( [ ( Expl, C)], Expl, C) :- !.
best_one( [ ( Expl1, C1)| Set], Expl, C) :-
  best_one( Set, Expl, C),
  C1 =< C, !.                                  % red cut !
best_one( [ ( Expl, C)| _], Expl, C).

ask( Q, C, _) :- known( Q, C), !.
ask( Q, C, Trace) :-
  askable( Q), !,
  write_list( [ 'How sure are you that ', Q,' is true ']),
  getanswer( A),
  treat( A, Q, C, Trace).

getanswer( A) :-
  repeat,
    write('(0..1/why)? '),
    read( A),
    nl,
  (A = why; number( A), A >= 0, A =< 1), !.

treat( why, Q, C, Trace) :- !,
  nl,
  display_trace( Trace),                       % see exercise 21
  ask( Q, C, Trace).
treat( C, Q, C, _) :- assert( known( Q, C)), !.
```

170

```
% display explanation:

display_expl( []).
display_expl( [ Q with C1 and C2 if true| Rules]) :- !,
  write_list( [ Q,
      ' was found as a fact with certainty ',
      C2, nl, nl]),
  display_expl( Rules).
display_expl( [ Q with C if useranswer| Rules]) :- !,
  write_list( [ Q,' was confirmed by the user with certainty ',
            C, nl, nl]),
  display_expl( Rules).
display_expl( [ Q with C1 and C2 if Body| Rules]) :-
  write_list( [ Q,' was derived with certainty ', C2,
        ' by rule:', nl]), .
  write_rule( Q, C1, Body), nl,
  display_expl( Rules).

write_rule( Q, C, B) :-
  write(' IF '),
  write_body( B), nl,                       % see exercise 19
  write_list([' THEN ', Q,' with certainty ', C, nl]).

min( X1, X2, X1) :- X1 =< X2.
min( X1, X2, X2) :- X1 > X2.
```

Prolog Built-in Procedures

his appendix provides an overview of standard Prolog built-in procedures that are redefined by most Prolog implementations and can not be redefined by the user. The relations between the arguments of a procedure and actions performed by the procedure are xplained. In this appendix, variable names beginning with the underscore character denote nput arguments that have to be instantiated before the procedure is called. If such an rgument is not instantiated the procedure may simply fail or cause a runtime error, epending on the implementation.

uilt-in procedures may be divided into several groups according to the tasks they perform: nput/output, arithmetic, comparison, control, metalogical operations and debugging. The najority of built-in procedures was already explained in the context of their use in the text f the book. The brief overview in this appendix lists them according to their alphabetical rder.

rg(_N,_T,A)   Term A is the __N-th argument of term __T.

ssert(_C)   Add the clause __C to the current program.

sserta(_C)   Like 'assert(__C)' except that the new clause becomes the first clause for the procedure concerned.

ssertz(_C)   Like 'assert(__C)' except that the new clause becomes the last clause for the procedure concerned.

tom(X)   X is an atom.

tomic(X)   X is a constant (an atom or a number).

agof(X,_G,B)   B is a list of all instances of X which satisfy goal(s) __G. In contrast to 'findall', it returns only instances of X for one instantiation of other variables in __G. If there is no such X the procedure fails.

call(_G)	Satisfy goal __G.
clause(_H,B)	Find a clause in the current program with head __H and body B.
close(_F)	Close file __F. If __F is the current input/output stream then switch the current input/output stream to the user's terminal.
consult(_F)	Read in the program from file __F by adding all syntactically correct clauses to the current program.
display(T)	Display term T on the screen.
fail	Immediately fail and invoke backtracking.
fileerrors	Enables writing of file error messages when input/output operations are performed.
findall(X,_G,L)	L is a list of all instances of X which satisfy goal(s) __G. In contrast to 'bagof', it also returns instances of X for different values of other variables in __G. If there is no such X, L is instantiated to the empty list.
functor(T,F,N)	T is a term with functor F and arity N. Either T must be instantiated or F and N must be instantiated.
get(C)	Read the next printing character from the current input stream and match C with its ASCII code.
get0(C)	Read the next character from the current input stream and match C with its ASCII code.
integer(X)	X is an integer.
X is _A	X is matched with the value of the evaluable arithmetic expression __A.
listing	Write the current program to the current output stream.
listing(_P)	Write the clauses of the procedure __P of the current program to the current output stream.
name(A,L)	L is the list of ASCII codes of the characters that compose the name of the constant A. At least one of A and L must be instantiated.
nl	Start writing in a new line on the current output stream.
nofileerrors	Disables writing of file error messages when input/output operations are performed. If an error occurs, the operation simply fails.
nonvar(X)	X is not an uninstantiated variable.
nospy(_P)	Remove spy-points from procedure(s) P.

174

not(_G)	If goal _G succeeds then not(_G) fails and vice versa.
notrace	Switch off the tracing mode of the interpreter.
op(_P,_T,_A)	Make atom _A an operator of type _T and precedence _P.
put(_C)	Write the character whose ASCII code is _C to the current output stream.
read(T)	Read the next term T, terminated with a period followed by at least one non-printing character, from the current input stream.
reconsult(_F)	Same as 'consult' except that all procedures from the current program that are also defined in file _F are removed before clauses from file _F are added to the current program.
repeat	Always succeeds, thus generating an unlimited number of alternatives for backtracking.
restore(_F)	Restore the program from file _F that was saved with the procedure 'save'.
retract(C)	Remove a clause that matches C from the current program.
save(_F)	Store the current program to file _F.
see(_F)	Switch the current input stream to file _F. If not yet opened open file _F for reading.
seeing(F)	F is matched with the name of the current input stream.
seen	Close the current input stream and switch it to the user's terminal.
setof(X,_G,S)	S is the set (list with no duplicates) of all instances of X such that satisfy goal(s) _G. In contrast to 'findall', it returns only instances of X for one instantiation of other variables in _G. If there is no such X the procedure fails.
skip(_C)	Read the characters from the current input stream until the character with ASCII code _C is reached.
spy(_P)	Set a spy point for the procedure(s) _P.
tab(_N)	Write _N spaces to the current output stream.
tell(_F)	Switch the current output stream to file _F. If not yet opened open file _F for writing (destroying its contents if it already exists).
telling(F)	F is matched with the name of the current output stream.

told	Close the current output stream and switch it to the user's terminal.
trace	Switch on the tracing mode of the interpreter.
true	Always succeeds, except on backtracking (in contrast to 'repeat').
var(X)	X is an uninstantiated variable.
write(T)	Write term T to the current output stream.
!	Cut always succeeds. When backtracking, it fails all the goals preceeding the cut and the parent goal.
_X < _Y	The value of evaluable arithmetic expression _X is less than the value of evaluable arithmetic expression _Y.
_X =< _Y	The value of evaluable arithmetic expression _X is less than or equal to the value of evaluable arithmetic expression _Y.
_X > _Y	The value of evaluable arithmetic expression _X is greater than the value of evaluable arithmetic expression _Y.
_X >= _Y	The value of evaluable arithmetic expression _X is greater than or equal to the value of evaluable arithmetic expression _Y
_X =:= _Y	The values of evaluable arithmetic expressions _X and _Y are equal.
_X =\= _Y	The values of evaluable arithmetic expressions _X and _Y are not equal.
X == Y	X and Y are literally identical.
X \== Y	X and Y are not literally identical.
X = Y	Match X and Y.
S =.. L	L is a list with the functor of structure S as the head and the list of arguments of S as the tail. At least one of S and L must be instantiated.

Standard Prolog Built-in Operators

```
:- op(1200, xfx, ':-' ).          % separator between the head and
                                   % the body of a clause
:- op(1200, xfx, --> ).           % production sign in definite clause
                                   % grammar notation
:- op(1200, fx,  ':-' ).          % beginning of a command
:- op(1200, fx,  '?-' ).          % beginning of a question
:- op(1100, xfy, ';' ).           % disjunction
:- op(1100, xf , ';' ).           % requirement for another solution
:- op(1000, xfy, ',' ).           % conjunction
:- op( 700, xfx, =  ).            % matching
:- op( 700, xfx, == ).            % literal equality
:- op( 700, xfx, \== ).           % literal non-equality
:- op( 700, xfx, is ).            % evaluation and assignment
:- op( 700, xfx, <  ).            % comparison (less than)
:- op( 700, xfx, >  ).            % comparison (greater than)
:- op( 700, xfx, =< ).            % comparison (less than or equal to)
:- op( 700, xfx, >= ).            % comparison (greater than or equal to)
:- op( 700, xfx, =:= ).           % comparison (equal values)
:- op( 700, xfx, =\= ).           % comparison (different values)
:- op( 500, yfx, +  ).            % addition
:- op( 500, yfx, -  ).            % subtraction
:- op( 500, fx,  +  ).            % positive sign
:- op( 500, fx,  -  ).            % negative sign
:- op( 400, yfx, *  ).            % multiplication
:- op( 400, yfx, /  ).            % division
:- op( 300, xfx, mod ).           % remainder of integer division
```

Appendix C

Printing Characters and Their ASCII Codes

char	code	char	code	char	code	char	code
!	33	:	58	S	83	l	108
"	34	;	59	T	84	m	109
#	35	<	60	U	85	n	110
$	36	=	61	V	86	o	111
%	37	>	62	W	87	p	112
&	38	?	63	X	88	q	113
'	39	@	64	Y	89	r	114
(	40	A	65	Z	90	s	115
)	41	B	66	[	91	t	116
*	42	C	67	\	92	u	117
+	43	D	68	]	93	v	118
,	44	E	69	^	94	w	119
-	45	F	70	_	95	x	120
.	46	G	71	`	96	y	121
/	47	H	72	a	97	z	122
0	48	I	73	b	98	{	123
1	49	J	74	c	99			124
2	50	K	75	d	100	}	125
3	51	L	76	e	101	~	126
4	52	M	77	f	102		
5	53	N	78	g	103		
6	54	O	79	h	104		
7	55	P	80	i	105		
8	56	Q	81	j	106		
9	57	R	82	k	107		

Appendix D

Glossary of Selected Terms Used in Prolog Programming

This glossary includes the main terms which are used in Prolog programming as well as some important terms of logic programming and artificial intelligence. Italic characters indicate that a term used in a definition is itself an entry in the glossary. In the case of synonyms, only the most commonly used term is explained, while synonyms are referred to the term. Prolog built-in procedures are not included in the glossary since they are described in Appendix A.

Abort: To stop; To stop the further *execution* of a *program*.

And: The symbol of the *logic operator* for *conjunction*.

Anonymous Variable: A *variable* used in place of an ordinary variable when its *name* and *value* are of no interest. Two anonymous variables in the same clause represent, in general, two different variables, thus an anonymous variable can not be used as a *shared variable*.

Answer: The *output* after a termination of *execution*. If the *goals* in a *question* were successfully satisfied, the answer also contains *values of the variables* in the question.

Antecedent: The *condition* part of a logical *implication*.

Argument: The collective name for *terms* in a *structure* that are enclosed in brackets and separated by commas. If a structure is constructed by using an *operator*, then its arguments are not enclosed in brackets. An argument of a *procedure* may be *input* or *output* or both.

Arithmetic Operator: An *operator* which constructs arithmetic *expressions*. It determines an operation on numbers such as addition, multiplication, etc. The value of an arithmetic expression can be obtained through its evaluation with an appropriate *arithmetic procedure*.

Arithmetic Predicate: Used as a synonym for an *arithmetic procedure*.

Arithmetic Procedure: A *built-in procedure* that enforces the evaluation of its *arguments,* which must be arithmetic *expressions* (for example 'is', '>', ' =:= '...).

Arity: The number of *arguments of a predicate or a functor.*

Artificial Intelligence: A field of computer science which deals with developing methods and tools for solving problems, understanding natural language, image processing, *logic programming, logical reasoning,* inductive learning, developing *expert systems,* etc. On the other hand, an important interest of artificial intelligence is to understand and model the principles of the human mind.

Assignment: Evaluating an arithmetic *expression* and *matching* the obtained value with a *variable* or a number. In Prolog, the *arithmetic procedure* 'is/2' is used for assignment.

Associativity: The way in which *operators* bind their *arguments* defined by the operator's *type.* An operator may be left or right associative or without associativity. Associativity is needed to avoid ambiguity when interpreting *terms* which contain several operators. In a term with several operators of the same *precedence* and defined as left associative, the leftmost operator binds stronger then others; analogously for right associativity. If an operator without associativity appears twice in a term, the desired structure must be explicitly determined by additional brackets.

Atom: A *constant* which is not a number. An atom is an inseparable unit in the Prolog source *code* (in mathematical logic atom stands for a positive literal).

Atomic Formula: A synonym for a *positive literal.*

Automatic Backtracking: See *backtracking.*

Automatic Programming: A field of computer science dealing with methods of automating the *programming* of computers in order to speed up the process of software development.

Backtracking: Part of the *execution* during which Prolog repeatedly attemps to *satisty* and *resatisfy* goals. Execution can not continue if there is no *clause* whose *head matches* the current *goal.* In such cases execution automatically returns to the last successfully matched goal and tries to match it in some other way.

Backtrack Point: Used as a synonym for *backtracking point.*

Backtracking Point: A clause marked by a *place-marker* from which an alternative *execution* path is possible when *backtracking.*

Binary: Having two *arguments.*

Binding of a Variable: See *variable binding.*

Body of a Clause: A sequence of *literals* called *goals, conjunctively* or *disjunctively* connected. The body of a clause is written on the right hand-side of the *operator* ':-'. It is also called the *condition* part of the *clause.* The body of a clause may also be empty.

Bound Variable: Used as a synonym for *instantiated variable* (in mathematical logic a bound variable is a quantified variable).

Boundary Condition: A condition in a *recursive procedure* needed to stop the *execution* of the procedure.

Box Representation: A representation of a Prolog *procedure* as a box with four ports: two entries (call and redo) and two exits (exit and fail). This representation is useful when *tracing* the *execution* of a procedure.

Box Model: See *box representation*.

Break: Temporary interruption of an *execution* initiated by the user.

Break Level: The level of a *break*. The number of nested breaks.

Built-in Operator: An *operator* already defined by the Prolog system. Prolog *implementations* may have slightly different sets of built-in operators. However, there is a standard set of built-in operators that appears in every Prolog implementation.

Built-in Predicate: See *built-in procedure*.

Built-in Procedure: A *procedure* that is already defined by the Prolog system and is available when *programming* in Prolog. Prolog *implementations* may have slightly different sets of built-in procedures.

Call: See *procedure call*. 'call' is usually a *built-in procedure*.

Circular Definition: A *procedure* that defines a *predicate* in terms of itself or with predicates that are defined with this same predicate without a *boundary condition*. This leads to *cycling* in the *execution*.

Circular Term: An *instance* of a *term* where a *variable* is *instantiated* to a *structure* containing the variable itself. See also *occurs check*.

Clausal Form: A form of *predicate calculus* where all formulas are in a disjunctive normal form (not containing quantifiers, *equivalence* nor *implication* operators) and all *variables* are implicitly *universally quantified*.

Clause: A part of the definition of a *procedure* terminated with a period. Clauses are of four types: *facts*, *rules*, *questions* and *commands*.

Closed World Assumption: The assumption that non-derivable *ground terms* are factually false. When *executing* a *program* Prolog assumes that everything that can be derived from a given program is true and everything else is false (although it cannot be proven that it is not true).

Code: *Program* statements written in accordance with the syntactic rules of a *programming language*.

Command: A *negative clause* having a non-empty *body*. A command is a part of a *program*. It is immediately executed and does not output *values of variables*.

Comment: In a Prolog *program*, a text to the right of ' % ' or between the symbols ' /* ' and ' */ '. A comment explains the *code* and is ignored by the *interpreter* or *compiler*.

Comparison Operators: *Predicates* defined as *operators* that can be used for comparing values of arithmetic *expressions*.

Compiler: A *program* that translates (compiles) users' programs into machine *code*.

Component: An *argument* of a *structure*.

Compound Object: Used as a synonym for *structure*.

Compound Term: A synonym for a *structure*.

Computation: See *execution*.

Conclusion: The *positive literal* on the left-hand side of the *operator* ':-' in a Prolog *clause*. It is also called *head of a clause*.

Condition: The condition part of a *clause* is the sequence of *literals* at the right-hand side of the *operator* ':-' in a Prolog clause. The condition part is also called *body of a clause*.

Conjunction: A sequence of *literals* connected by the *logic operator* 'and'. A conjunction is *true* if and only if all its literals are true.

Consequent: The *conclusion* part of a logical *implication*.

Constant: An *atom* or a number. A constant denotes a specific individual.

Consulting: Reading in Prolog *procedures* from files.

Control Predicates: Used as a synonym for *control procedures*.

Control Procedures: *Built-in procedures* that can be used for controling the *execution* (for example cut, fail, repeat etc.).

Conventional Language: Usually used as a synonym for *procedural language*.

Current Database: See *current program*.

Current Input Stream: The *input stream* from which the *program* is currently reading data. By default, the current input stream is the user's terminal.

Current Output Stream: The *output stream* to which the *program* is currently writing data. By default, the current output stream is the user's terminal.

Current Program: The set of Prolog *clauses* currently accessible for *execution* by the Prolog *interpreter*.

Cut: A *control procedure* denoted by '!'.

Cycling: An endless loop in *execution* usually caused by a *recursive call* without a *boundary condition*. Execution is aborted when available memory is exhausted.

Data Object: A syntactic construct for representing data. It can be a *simple object* or a *compound object*.

Data Structure: A synonym for *data object*.

Database: A set of *facts* that can be used for *answering* user's *questions*.

Database Interpretation: Interpretation of a Prolog *program* as a *database*.

Debugging: The process of discovering and removing semantical errors (bugs) in a *program*.

Declarative Interpretation: The interpretation of Prolog *programs* as definitions of *relations* between *objects*.

Declarative Language: A programming language in which programs are written by stating what is to be done rather than prescribing how to do it.

Declarative Meaning: See *declarative interpretation*.

Declarative Reading: See *declarative interpretation*.

Declarative Semantics: See *declarative interpretation*.

Deductive Database: A set of *facts* and *rules* that can be used for *answering* user's *questions*.

Definite Clause Grammar: A Prolog extension of contex-free grammars, allowing arguments and Prolog calls at the right-hand sides of *grammar rules*. The left-hand side of a grammar rule consists of a non-terminal, optionally followed by a sequence of terminals, while the right-hand side of the rule contains a sequence of terminals and nonterminals, *extra conditions* and possibly a *cut* symbol, which limits the possible derivations.

Depth-first Search: A strategy for searching graphs in which alternative paths are tried only after the current search path is explored to the end (if it has one).

Derived Goal: Successfuly *satisfied goal*.

Difference-list: A *list* notation constructed as a difference of two lists giving efficient access to the right end of the list. The second list in a difference-list notation represents the right end part of the original list.

Disjunction: A sequence of *literals* connected with the *logic operator* 'or'. A disjunction is *true* if at least one literal is true.

Double Recursion: A *recursive procedure* with two *recursive calls*.

Edinburgh Prolog Syntax: A standard Prolog syntax adopted by many *implementations*.

Empty List: A *list* without elements, denoted by ' [ ] '.

Endless Loop: See *cycling*.

Equality Operators: *Comparison operators* which state that their *arguments* are equivalent. There are different kinds of equality in Prolog. Arguments may be equivalent if they *match* or if they are literally identical. The third kind of equality is between arithmetic *expressions* whose values are identical.

Equivalence: A logical statement which states that two *expressions* are both *true* or both *false*.

Evaluable Predicate: Used as a synonym for a *built-in procedure*.

Execution: A sequence of actions which the Prolog *interpreter* performs on *facts* and *rules* of the *program* in order to find a solution to a given problem, i.e. in order to *satisfy* a sequence of *goals* in a *question*.

Executing Goals: A process performed by a Prolog *interpreter* of *satisfying goals* in a sequence from left to the right. See also *execution*.

Existential Quantification: *Quantification* of a logical *expression* on a *variable* stating that the expression holds for at least one *object* that the variable denotes.

Expert System: A computer system that achieves performance comparable to that of a human expert at solving problems in a certain domain. It utilizes a large amount of domain specific knowledge and must be able to explain and argue its conclusions. An expert system is usually built with *artificial intelligence* tools and techniques.

Expression: A *term* or a sequence of terms connected by *logic operators* (for logical expression) or *arithmetic operators* (for arithmetic expression).

Extra Conditions: Conditions in Prolog clauses written in a *definite clause grammar* notation, that limit possible derivations to those that satisfy these conditions.

Extra-logical Predicate: A *predicate* defined by a *built-in procedure* that performs some specific operation and does not represent a logical *relation*. Extra-logical predicates are used for *input/output* operations, for adding and removing *clauses* from a Prolog *program* and for communicating with the underlying operating system.

Fact: A Prolog *clause* with an empty *body*. It describes a property or a *relation* between *objects* that is unconditionally true.

Fail: A *built-in procedure* that always immediately fails. Also the name of the exit port in the *box representation* used when the *execution* of a given *procedure* is not successful.

Failure: The termination of an unsuccesful *execution* of a *goal*.

False: A *logical value*. A logical statement may either have the value *true* or false.

First-order Logic: See *first-order predicate calculus*.

First-order Predicate Calculus: *Predicate calculus* in which *literals* may not be *arguments* of other literals. The arguments of literals must be *terms*.

Free Variable: Used as a synonym for *uninstantiated variable*. See also *unbound variable* (in mathematical logic a free variable is an unquantified variable).

Function: Usually used as a synonym for a *functor* (Prolog has no functions in the mathematical sense, but it can simulate a n-*ary* function with a (n+1)-ary *predicate*).

Functor: The *name* of a Prolog *structure* with an associated *arity*. Syntactically a *predicate* is a functor (in mathematical logic a functor is equivalent to a function). 'functor/3' is also a *built-in procedure*.

Global Variable: A *variable* whose *lexical scope* is the whole *program*. Prolog has no global variables.

Goal: A *literal* in the *body of a Prolog clause* that the Prolog *interpreter* tries to *satisfy* when *executing* a given *clause*. A goal is also called a *procedure call*.

Grammar Rule: A rule of the form 'L -> R', meaning that in generating an element of the language L can be replaced by R.

Green Cut: A *cut* that can be removed without affecting the procedural correctness of the *procedure*.

Ground Goal: A *goal* that does not contain any *variables*.

Ground Instance: An *instance* that contains no *uninstantiated variables*.

Ground Term: A *term* that contains no *variables*.

Head of a Clause: The *positive literal* at the left-hand side of the *operator* ':-' in a Prolog *clause*. It is also called the *conclusion* part of a clause. The head of a clause may also be empty.

Head of a List: The first element of a *list*.

Horn Clause: A logic *implication* in which the *antecedent* consists of a *conjunction of positive literals* and the *consequent* of at most one *positive literal*. It is the basis for Prolog *clauses*. Prolog clauses may also contain *disjunction* and *negative literals* in the *body of a clause*.

If-then Rules: An *inference rule* containing a condition and a conclusion and stating that the conclusion is *true* if the condition is. Prolog *clauses* can be viewed as if-then rules.

Identity: Literal equality. One of the *equality operators* in Prolog, usually denoted by ' == '.

Implementation: Realisation of a certain algorithm on a computer. Usually used as a synonym for a version of a Prolog *interpreter* or *compiler*.

Implication: A logical statement of the form 'A = > B', in which A is called the *antecedent* or the *condition*, and B the *consequent* or the *conclusion*; ' = > ' is the implication *operator*. An implication is *true* if the antecedent is *false* or the consequent true.

Inference Mechanism: A mechanism for logical reasoning.

Inference Rule: A rule used by an *inference mechanism* to derive consequences (i.e. a goal) from given axioms (i.e. a program).

Infinite Loop: See *cycling*.

Infinite Term: See *circular term*.

Infix Notation: A notation in which the *operator* is written between its two *arguments*, without brackets.

Input: Data given to a *program*.

Input Argument: An *argument* of a *procedure* whose *value* is already determined at the time of a *procedure call*.

Input Stream: A *stream* from which a *program* reads data.

Instance: A *term* with (partially) *instantiated variables*.

Instantiated Variable: A *variable* with a certain *value*.

Instantiation: The *values of variables* in a *term*.

Interactive Program: A *program* which communicates with a user via a terminal.

Interpret: To *execute* without translating or *compiling* the original *code*.

Interpreter: A program that recognizes the *code* of a *program* and *interprets* it.

Iterative Method: A method which involves repeating the same basic action over and over again until the desired objective is achieved.

Joint Variable: See *shared variable*.

Knowledge-base: A substantial part of an *expert system*, containing knowledge about the domain, usually in the form of *facts* and *rules*.

Left Associativity: See *associativity*.

Left-to-right Rule: A rule of *executing goals* in a list of goals to be *satisfied*.

Length of a List: Number of elements in a *list*.

Lexical Scope: A way of interpreting the same *name* in different parts of a *program*. In Prolog, the lexical scope of *variables* is limited to a single *clause*. This means that the same variable name in two different clauses denotes two different variables. The lexical scope of *procedures* is a whole program, i.e. the same procedure name and *arity* represent the same procedure throughout the program.

LIPS: Abbreviation for 'Logical Inferences Per Second'. A measure for the speed of *execution* of Prolog *programs* on different Prolog implementations.

List: An ordered sequence of items which may be arbitrary Prolog *terms*. A list is the most important Prolog data structure written in a special notation. Elements of a list are enclosed in square brackets and separated by commas.

Listing: Displaying a *program* on a screen or on paper. Usually it is a *built-in procedure*.

List Difference: See *difference-list*.

Literal: A part of a logic *expression*, constructed from a *predicate name* and a list of *arguments*, optionally preceeded by a *negation* sign. A literal may thus be *positive* or *negative*. Interpretation of a literal assigns it a *logical value*.

Local Variable: A *variable* with a limited *lexical scope*. In Prolog each variable is local to the *clause* in which it occurs.

Logic Operator: An *operator* which determines logical operation between *literals* such as *conjunction*, *disjunction* and *negation*.

Logic Programming: A field of computer science which deals with *programming languages* and techniques based on mathematical logic.

Logical Value: A value assigned to a logical *expression*. Logical value may be either *true* or *false*.

Main Procedure: See *top level procedure*.

Main Program: A *program* containing the *top level procedures* and conections between *modules* of a whole program.

Mapping of a List: Converting one *list* to another by applying some transformation to each *element of a list*.

Marker: See *place-marker*.

Matching: A process by which the Prolog *interpreter* tries to make two *terms* identical. Matching is an efficient implementation of *unification*. It usually differs from unification in allowing a *variable* to get *instantiated* to a *term* containing that same variable. See also *occurs check*.

189

Meta-variable: A *variable* which stands for a *goal* in a *body of a clause.*

Metalogical Predicate: A *predicate* defined by a *built-in procedure* denoting a *relation* between constructs of a Prolog *program* which is not covered in *first-order predicate calculus.*

Mnemonic Name: A *name* which clearly shows what it is intended to stands for. Mnemonic names improve readability of *programs.*

Module: A part of a *program* for solving a certain (kind of) problem(s), usually saved on a separate file.

Modular Programming: A way of *programming* where the problem is partitioned into sub-problems which are then solved by special *programs* called *modules.*

Most General Instatiation: See *most general match.*

Most General Match: An *instatiation* of two *terms* after *matching*, with *variables* instantiated only to the extent to make the two terms identical.

Name: A continuous sequence of letters, digits and underscore characters which starts with an uppercase letter or underscore for a *variable* and a lowercase letter for an *atom.*

Negation: Logical statement stating that an *expression* is not *true.*

Negation As Failure: Implementation of a kind of *negation* in Prolog. The negation of a *goal* succeeds if the goal *fails* and vice versa. Prolog does not support strict logical negation.

Negation Sign: See *not.*

Negative Clause: A Prolog *clause* with no *head.* There are two types of negative clauses: *questions* and *commands.*

Negative Literal: A negated *literal.* A literal with a *negation sign.*

Non-deterministic Execution: *Execution* for which it is not known in advance at which *clause* of *procedures* it will *succeed.*

Non-ground Term: A *term* that is not *ground*, i.e. a term which contains also some uninstantiated variables.

Non-printing Character: A character that does not cause a mark to appear on the terminal's display but cause a certain action to be carried out (as for example jumping to the beginning of a new line). Opposite of *printing characters.* ASCII codes of non-printing characters are under 32 inclusively.

Not: *Logic operator* for *negation.* Usually a *built-in procedure* implementing *negation as failure.*

Object: An individual item.

Occurs Check: A check whether a given *variable* appears in a given *term*. This operation is time consuming and therefore usually not included in *matching*.

Open World Assumption: The opposite of the *closed world assumption*.

Operator: A *unary* or a *binary functor* used in *prefix, postfix* or *infix* notation without brackets. An operator is defined by its *name, precedence* and *type*.

Or: The *logic operator* for *disjunction*.

Output: Data written by a *program* on a screen or file.

Output Argument: An *argument* of a *procedure* whose value is determined after the successful *execution* of the procedure.

Output Stream: A *stream* to which a *program* writes data.

Parameter: A synonym for an *argument*.

Parent Goal: The *goal* that matched the *head of the clause*, in whose body the *execution* is currently trying to *satisfy* or *resatisfy* a certain goal.

Place-marker: During the *execution* a pointer to the *clause* whose *head* was last *matched* with the given *goal*.

Positive Literal: A non-negative *literal*.

Postfix Notation: Writing a unary *operator* after its *argument*, without brackets.

Precedence: The strength with which an *operator* binds its *arguments*. This notion is needed to avoid ambiguity when interpreting *expressions* which contain several operators without using brackets. The lower the precedence, the stronger the operator binds its arguments.

Predefined Operator: See *built-in operator*.

Predefined Predicate: Used as a synonym for a *built-in procedure*.

Predefined Procedure: See *built-in procedure*.

Predicate: A formal representation of a *relation*. It is determined by a *name* and an *arity*. A predicate is defined by a *procedure*.

Predicate Calculus: A mathematical logic formalism for expressing assertions and checking the consequences of given assertions. Predicate calculus uses *variables, constants, functors* for constructing *terms, predicates* for constructing *positive literals* (also called atomic formulas), the *logic operators* 'and' (*conjunction*), 'or' (*disjunction*), 'not' (*negation*), '=>' (*implication*) and '<=>' (*equivalence*) for constructing logic *expressions,* and *universal* and *existential quantifications*.

Predicate Logic: See *predicate calculus*.

Prefix Notation: Writing a unary *operator* in front of its *argument*, without using brackets.

Principal Functor: The *functor* at the root of the tree representing a given *structure*, i.e. the functor with the highest *precedence*.

Printing Character: A character that causes a mark to appear on the terminal's display. Opposite of a *non-printing character*. ASCII codes of printing characters are above 32.

Priority: A synonym for *precedence*.

Procedural Interpretation: The *interpretation* of a Prolog *procedure* as a sequence of *clauses* whose *bodies* are in turn interpreted as sequences of *goals*. In contrast with the *declarative interpretation*, the order of clauses in goals is significant. The procedural interpretation defines how Prolog will actually solve a given problem.

Procedural Language: A *programming language* which can be only proceduraly interpreted: *programs* define how to solve a given problem by an ordered sequence of actions.

Procedural Meaning: See *procedural interpretation*.

Procedural Reading: See *procedural interpretation*.

Procedural Semantics: See *procedural interpretation*.

Procedure: A set of *clauses* that define the same *predicate*, i.e. clauses with the same predicate *name* and *arity* in their *heads*.

Procedure Box: See *box representation*.

Procedure Call: A call for *satisfying* a *goal* in a *rule* or a *question*. The goal is to be matched with the *head of a clause* of the appropriate *procedure*.

Program: A sequence of *clauses* in a given syntax that is understood by an *interpreter* or a *compiler*. A Prolog program consists of sets of clauses grouped into *procedures*.

Prolog: A programming language based on mathematical logic. PROLOG stands for 'PROgramming in LOGic'. It is the basic language in the field of *logic programming*.

Prompt: A sequence of characters that an interactive program displays on a screen in order to show the user that it is ready to accept input.

Pure Prolog: Prolog without any *built-in procedures*.

Quantificator: A quantificator is either *existential* or *universal*. It determines the quantity of possible *values of a variable*.

Query: Synonym for a *question*.

Question: A Prolog *clause* used for defining a problem to be solved by a given *program*. It consists of a list of *conjunctively* and/or *disjunctively* connected *literals* called *goals* which Prolog has to *satisfy*. A question is also called a *query*. It differs from a *command* in that it causes output of *values* of *variables*.

Recursion: A technique whereby a concept is defined in terms of itself, with a *boundary condition*.

Recursive Call: A *procedure call* where a *procedure* calls itself.

Recursive Data Structure: A data *structure* defined in terms of itself.

Recursive Procedure: A *procedure* defining a *predicate* in terms of itself together with a *boundary condition*.

Red Cut: A *cut* that can not be removed without affecting the procedural correctness of the *procedure*.

Relation: In mathematical logic a set of n-tuples of *objects*.

Relational Database: A *database* in which data is represented in the form of *relations* without using variables.

Resatisfy: To *satisfy* in another way.

Resolution: A proof method in mathematical logic.

Right Associativity: See *associativity*.

Rule: A Prolog *clause* constructed from a *condition* (a non-empty *body)* and a *conclusion* (the *head of a clause)*. A rule states that a conclusion is *true* if a condition is.

Runtime Error: An error that occurs during the *execution*.

Safe Use of Cut: The use of *green cut*.

Satisfy: Prove that the *goal* is *true* and under which conditions it is. The goal is satisfied if it *matches* the *head of some clause* in a *program* and if all the goals in a *body of that clause* are satisfied. Conditions under which the goal is true are determined by the *values of variables*.

Scope: See *lexical scope*.

Selector: A *rule* for selecting certain data from a *database*.

Shared Variable: A *variable* that appears more than once in a *clause*.

Simple Condition: A *condition* containing only one *literal*.

Simple Object: Used as a synonym for a *simple term*.

Simple Term: A *constant* or a *variable.*

Solution: A list of *values of variables* that were *instantiated* during an *execution.*

Spy Point: A *procedure* whose at which the *tracing mode* of the Prolog *interpreter* is switched on during the *execution.*

Stack Overflow: The *runtime error* when *execution* exhausts the available computer memory. Frequently caused by a *recursive definition* without an appropriate *boundary condition.*

Standard Predicate: Used as a synonym for a *standard built-in procedure.*

Standard Built-In Procedure: A *built-in procedure* in most of Prolog *implementations.*

Standard Prolog: Used as a synonym for *Edinburgh Prolog.*

Stepwise Refinement: A process in a *top-down* design of a *program* where each problem is partitioned in subproblems, and each subproblem solved in turn.

Stopping Condition: See *boundary condition.*

Stream: A device or file for receiving (*output stream*) or supplying (*input stream*) a sequence of characters that a Prolog *program* will write or read, respectively.

String: In Prolog, a *list* of integers which are ASCII codes of characters. Also an arbitrary sequence of characters enclosed in double quotes (").

Structure: A *term* consisting of a *functor* and a sequence of *arguments* separated by commas and enclosed in brackets. Arguments may be arbitrary Prolog terms.

Subgoal: A *goal* in the *body of a clause* whose *head* has *matched* the current goal. The opposite of *parent goal.*

Subterm: A *term* which is an *argument* in another term.

Success: A succesful *execution*, a successful *satisfaction* of a list of *goals* in a *question.*

Symbolic Programming: Writing *programs* that manipulate with symbolic names in contrast with operating with numbers.

Syntax Error: An error that can be detected by a *compiler* or an *interpreter* when the program code is not correct according to the syntax rules of the *programming language.*

System Predicate: See *built-in procedure.*

System Procedure: See *built-in procedure.*

Tail of a List: The remainder of a *list* after the first element is removed.

Term: Any Prolog data object. A term is either a *simple term* or a *structure*. *Arguments* of a structure may again be arbitrary terms.

Theorem-prover Interpretation: An *interpretation of a Prolog program* as a set of axioms, a *question* as a theorem and the *trace* of the *execution* of a *program* as a proof of a theorem.

Top-down Approach: A problem solving method beginning with the whole problem and continuing with the *stepwise refinement* of the problem.

Top Level Predicates: See *top level procedures*.

Top Level Procedures: *Procedures* to be called for solutions to a whole problem or the main parts of a problem. In a *top-down approach* they are written first.

Trace: The sequence of actions performed by the Prolog *interpreter* when *executing* a *program*. Prolog interpeter keeps the trace in a memory in order to enable *backtracking* when necessary.

Tracing: Following the way Prolog *executes* a given *program*.

Tracing Mode: Mode of *execution* where the *trace* of the execution is displayed.

True: The *logical value* that is assigned to a succesfully *satisfied goal*.

Truth Value: See *logical value*.

Type of an Operator: Defines whether an *operator* can be written in *prefix*, *postfix* or *infix* notation (without brackets) and what its *associativity* is.

Unary: Having one *argument*.

Unbound Variable: In logic programming used as a synonym for *uninstantiated variable*. In mathematical logic a synonym for *free variable*.

Unification: In mathematical logic the process of making two *terms* identical by *instantiating* their *variables*. *Matching* is an efficient but usually not complete implementation of unification.

Uninstantiated Variable: A *variable* that does not currently refer to any *value*. The opposite of an *instantiated variable*.

Unit clause: A synonym for a *fact*.

Universal Quantification: A *quantification* of a *variable* in a logical *expression* which states that the statement holds for all *objects* which the variable stands for.

Unsafe Use of Cut: The use of *red cut*.

Value of a Variable: A *term* to which a *variable* is *instantiated*. The value of a variable can be more or less specified: a variable can be *uninstantiated*, partially *instantiated* (i.e. containing other variables), or completely instantiated (i.e. *ground*).

Variable: A *name* beginning with a capital letter or an underscore character used to denote an arbitrary individual. During the *execution* of a Prolog *program* the *value of a variable* can become more specified, but can not be changed (except when *backtracking*).

Variable Binding: See *value of a variable*.

Variant of a Clause: A *clause* with new, renamed *variables* in order to make the clause independent of the original one.

Bibliography

Arity Corporation (1986), *"An Introduction to Arity/Prolog"*.

Arity Corporation (1986), *"Building Arity/Prolog Application"*.

Arity Corporation (1986), *"The Arity/Prolog Programming Language"*.

Bratko, I. (1986), *"Prolog Programming for Artificial Intelligence"*. Addison-Wesley.

Briggs, J. (1983), *"Introduction to micro-Prolog for the Sinclair ZX Spectrum"*. Sinclair Research Limited, Cambridge.

Burnham, W.D., Hall, A.R. (1985), *"Prolog Programming and Applications"*. Macmillan Education Ltd.

Clark, K.L., McCabe, F.G. (1984), *"micro-Prolog : Programming in Logic"*. Prentice Hall.

Clocksin, W.F., Mellish, C.S. (1981), *"Programming in Prolog"*. Springer Verlag.

Coelho, H., Cotta, J.C., Pereira, L.M. (1982), *"How to Solve It With Prolog"*. Lisboa.

Ennals, R. (1984), *"Beginning micro-Prolog"*. Ellis Horwood Ltd.

Giannesini, F., Kanoui, H., Pasero, R., van Caneghem, M. (1986), *"Prolog"*. Addison-Wesley.

Hogger, C.J. (1984), *"Introduction to Logic Programming"*. Accademic Press.

Kowalski, R. (1979), *"Logic for Problem Solving"*. North Holland.

Li D. (1984), *"A Prolog Database System"*. Research Studies Press.

Lloyd, J.W. (1984), *"Foundations of Logic Programming"*. Springer Verlag.

LPA ltd (1983), *"Sinclair ZX Spectrum micro-Prolog Primer"*.

Malpas, J. (1987), *"Prolog: A Relational Language and its Applications"*. Prentice Hall.

McCabe, F.G., Clark, K.L., Steel, B.D. (1984), *"micro-Prolog 3.1 Programmer's Reference Manual"*. Logic Programming Associates LTD.

Micro-AI (1983), *"Prolog 86 User's Guide and Reference Manual"*.

Pereira, F., Warren, D., Bowen, D., Pereira, L.M. (1983), *"C-Prolog User's Manual"*. SRI International, Menlo Park.

Pereira, L.M., Pereira, F., Warren, D. (1978), *"User's Guide for DEC-10 Prolog"*. Dept. of Artificial Intelligence, University of Edinburgh.

Sterling, L., Shapiro, E. (1986), *"The Art of Prolog – Advanced Programming Techniques"*. MIT Press.

Townsend, C. (1987), *"Introduction to Turbo Prolog"*. Sybex.

Walker, A., McCord, M., Sowa, J., Wilson, W. (1987), *"Knowledge Systems and Prolog"*. Addison-Wesley.